100 Winning Bridge Tips
for the Improving Player

Learning from bitter experience at the bridge table
is a slow, painful, and often costly business. Most of
us turn gray on the head and long in the tooth
before absorbing the knowledge needed to play a
competent game of bridge.

There is no need to despair, for help is at hand.
This book by the well-known author Ron Klinger is
written for improving players with the express aim
of cutting down on the agony and speeding up the
process of learning. The 100 winning tips cover
specific situations in bidding, play and defense. This
book addresses the problems that arise over and
over again in everyday play and provides a painless
substitute for experience. The idea is to learn how
to deal with all the common problems in advance,
so that they will not appear unfamiliar and
frightening when you meet them at the bridge table.

Those who apply themselves seriously to this
book will soon find their game lifted to a much
higher level.

Standard American Edition

100
WINNING
BRIDGE
TIPS

for the Improving Player

RON KLINGER

A Master Bridge Series title
in conjunction with Peter Crawley

Houghton Mifflin Company
Boston • New York • London

To Kurt and Hertha

Copyright © 1987 by Ron Klinger
All rights reserved

For information about permission to reproduce selections from
this book, write to Permissions, Houghton Mifflin Company,
215 Park Avenue South, New York, New York 10003.
The right of Ron Klinger to be identified as the author has been
asserted by him in accordance with the Copyright, Designs and
Patents Act of 1988.

Library of Congress Cataloging-in-Publication Data

Klinger, Ron. 100 winning bridge tips for the improving player /
Ron Klinger.
p. cm. — (A master bridge series title)
Reprint. Previously published: London : V. Gollancz in
association with P. Crawley, 1987.
Includes index.
ISBN 0-395-62887-3
1. Contract bridge. I. Title. II. Title: One hundred winning
bridge tips for the improving player. III. Series: Master bridge
series.
[GV1282.3.K615 1992]
795.4'15 — dc20   92-5941
CIP

Printed in the United States of America
BP 10 9 8 7 6 5 4 3 2

Contents

Introduction

A great deal of bridge expertise comes from experience. No matter how much book learning you may do, there is no substitute for the 'hands-on' background of what actually takes place at the table. With a storehouse of practical knowledge, a player is well-equipped to cope with recurring themes and new problems.

The expert player has this invaluable comprehensive background and very rarely comes across a situation or theme that is not well worn into the memory tracts. But what of the improving player who has not 'been there, done that'? It may be years before all the relevant positions arise at the table.

We need to reduce this time factor and speed up the process of learning. This collection of 100 practical tips on all areas of the game will stand the reader in good stead for solving the day to day challenges in regular play. The emphasis is on constant recurring worries and how to solve them. The tips are framed not as vague generalities but in specific how-to-do-it terms. Some of the material has been gleaned from earlier sources, some will not be found elsewhere and comes from actual situations faced in tournaments or rubber bridge settings. All of it is important for success and if the reader can apply just 25% of the recommendations, there is no doubt that results are bound to improve measurably. The visible proof will appear with better scores and more winning sessions.

It's a lot of fun to play bridge but even more fun when you play and win. A winning session is a great tonic and psychological boost. *100 Winning Bridge Tips* will give you the winning feeling, the euphoria of victory more often. Actually there are far more than 100 tips in this book. In many cases there is additional advice in the text and discussion and extra tips when the solutions to the problems are presented. All of these extra tips can further enhance your skills and produce a more polished and successful player.

Ron Klinger
1987

TIPS 1-15: The Rule of 1 to the Rule of 40

TIP 1:

The Rule of 1: **When there is just one trump out higher than yours, it is normally best to leave it out.**

When your opponents have the best trump, it is bound to score sooner or later and there is usually no need to let them score it early. To eliminate their top trump costs you two trumps and gives up the initiative. You may not be able to afford either.

WEST	EAST	
♠ A K Q 7 3	♠ 6	West is in 5♣ and ruffs the
♡ 5	♡ J 6 4 2	second heart. The ♣A-K sees
◇ A K	◇ 9 7 5 2	North show out on the second
♣ A K 6 4 2	♣ 8 7 5 3	round. What now?

West must abandon trumps and start on the spades, planning to ruff two spades in dummy to ensure the game. If West were to eliminate their top trump, dummy would have just one trump left and West would fail if either opponent held five or more spades.

WEST	EAST	
♠ A 2	♠ J 6	West is in the fine contract of
♡ 9 7 5 3 2	♡ A K 6 4	6♡ and receives the ♠K lead.
◇ A 2	◇ K Q J 7 6 5	West takes the ♠A and cashes the
♣ A J 5 4	♣ 8	♡A and K. North shows out on the second round of trumps. What now?

It would be a beginners' error to play a third trump, allowing the opponents to cash a spade. West must start on diamonds and hope that South began with at least two diamonds so that the spade loser can be discarded on the third diamond.

WEST	EAST	
♠ A K 2·	♠ J 6	West again has reached a good
♡ K 9 7 5 3 2	♡ A 6	6♡ (even though 6◇ is superior,
◇ A 2	◇ K Q J 7 6 5	6♡ is respectable) and North
♣ A 6	♣ Q 8 3	leads a low spade-J-Q-A. All follow to the ♡A and K. How should West continue?

Where dummy has a long solid suit to run and no outside entry, you must ignore the Rule of 1 and draw opponents' top trump. Otherwise, they may ruff in and prevent your using all the tricks available in dummy. Play a third round of hearts.

TIP 2:

The Rule of 2: **When you are missing two non-touching honours, it is normally superior to finesse first for their *lower* honour.**

WEST	EAST	
7 6 5	A Q 10	If you need three tricks or the maximum possible, finesse the 10 first, not Q.
WEST	EAST	
8 7 6 4 2	K J 10 5 3	You lead the 2 and North follows with the 9. Do you finesse the 10 or K?

If South has A-Q, your play is immaterial. If the A and Q are split, either finesse is a 50% chance. It is correct to finesse the J, since this gains when North has Q9 *and also* when North has AQ9.

When one of the two missing honours is the 10 the rule will not apply, as one does not normally finesse for a 10 on the first round.

When the two missing honours are the A and J, it is normal to finesse for the J on the second round, just in case the J drops before the finesse is necessary. For example:

WEST	EAST	
K 7 6 4	Q 10 9 3	It would be an error to lead low to the 10 first. Lead the 3 to the K and finesse the 10 on the next round.

However if only one finesse can be taken, it is correct to finesse for the J first. For example:

WEST	EAST	
7	K Q 10 5 4 2	The best chance to lose just one trick is to lead the 7 to the 10.

In unusual cases you need not follow the Rule of 2. For example, if you need only two tricks from AQ10 opposite xxx and cannot afford to lose the lead, finesse the Q. Likewise, if you have to keep a specific opponent off lead:

WEST	EAST	
♠ 8 7 6 4 3 2	♠ K J 10 5	West is in 4♠ on a low club lead
♡ K 5 3	♡ 7 6 4	to the Q and A. How should
◇ 8 2	◇ A K Q J 3	West proceed?
♣ A J	♣ 6	

West's best chance is to lead a trump and play dummy's K if North plays the 9. This works if North began with A-9 and even if North started with AQ9, North cannot do West damage in hearts, which can be discarded on the diamonds. If you finesse the J and find South with Q-singleton, a heart through the K may spell defeat.

TIP 3:

The Rule of 3: **On a competitive part score deal, with the points roughly equal between your side and theirs, once the bidding has reached the 3-level, tend to defend rather than bid on (unless your side has 9 trumps.)**

WEST
♠ K J 6
♡ J 6 3
◇ A K·J 8 6 2
♣ 8

Suppose the bidding has gone:

Dealer South: Both vulnerable

SOUTH	WEST	NORTH	EAST
1♠	2◇	No	No
Dble	?		

What would you do as West?

There is no reason to take any action here, so you pass and the bidding now continues:

SOUTH	WEST	NORTH	EAST
1♠	2◇	No	No
Dble	No	3♣	No
No	?		

What would you do now?

They seem likely to make 3♣ but as there is no evidence that your side has nine trumps, you should sell out at the 3-level. Had North bid 2♡ or 2♠, then you should compete to 3◇, but if you bid 3◇ over 3♣ you deserve a layout like this:

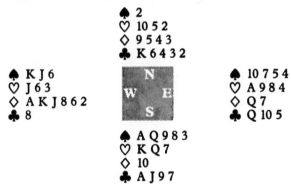

```
                    ♠ 2
                    ♡ 10 5 2
                    ◇ 9 5 4 3
                    ♣ K 6 4 3 2
♠ K J 6                             ♠ 10 7 5 4
♡ J 6 3                             ♡ A 9 8 4
◇ A K J 8 6 2                       ◇ Q 7
♣ 8                                 ♣ Q 10 5
                    ♠ A Q 9 8 3
                    ♡ K Q 7
                    ◇ 10
                    ♣ A J 9 7
```

North would lead the ♠2 against 3◇ and the play would go: ♠A, ♠3 ruffed, ♣ to the A, ♠9 ruffed. Heart exit and West must go two down. Interchange the ◇3 and the ◇Q and North should double 3◇.

When should you compete above them at the 3-level?

1. When you have 9 or more trumps your way.

2. When your side has a definite and clear strength advantage, e.g. 23 HCP v. 17 HCP. Even with both of these assets, do not compete a partscore to the 4-level.

WEST	WEST	NORTH	EAST	SOUTH
♠ A J 8 7 6 4		No	No	1◇
♡ 7	1♠	Dble*	2♠	3♡
◇ K J 3	?			
♣ 6 4 3			*For takeout	

What should West do now?

West knows East-West have at least nine trumps and with a shortage in hearts and well-placed diamonds, West has a clearcut 3♠ bid. Some would bid even 4♠, but there is nothing to say that North-South intend bidding 4♡.

EAST	WEST	NORTH	EAST	SOUTH
♠ K Q 7		No	No	1◇
♡ J 10 3	1♠	2♡	2♠	3♡
◇ A 9 5 2	No	No	?	
♣ 7 6 3				

What should East do?

The evidence is that East-West do not have nine trumps (West declined to bid 3♠ despite East's support). East has no shortage and thus no ruffing values and has reasonable defensive strength. East should pass 3♡.

EAST	WEST	NORTH	EAST	SOUTH
♠ 8 2	No	1◇	No	1♠
♡ 9 7	No	2♠	No	No
◇ 9 4 3	Dble	3♠	?	
♣ K Q J 8 7 6				

What should East do?

West's double was purely competitive, aimed at pushing North-South one level higher, and West has succeeded in that objective. With a decent hand, West would have bid earlier. East must pass—it is unsound to compete at the 4-level.

TIP 4:

The Rule of 4:   **Avoid giving support for partner's 5-card suit if a superior 4-4 fit might be available.**

A good 4-4 fit can enable you to make extra tricks by utilising the 5-3, 5-4 or 6-4 side fit for discards.

WEST	EAST
♠ A Q 5 2	♠ K 8 7 6
♡ K Q 8 7 6	♡ A J 3
◇ A 3	◇ J 5
♣ 5 2	♣ 9 8 7 4

If West opens 1♡, showing a 5-card major, East ought to respond 1♠, not 2♡. This will allow 4♠ to be reached which can make 11 tricks if spades are 3-2, while 10 tricks is the normal limit in hearts. If spades are 4-1, 4♠ may still succeed, while 4♡ will almost surely fail.

WEST	EAST
♠ K J 8 7 6	♠ A Q 3
♡ A Q 5 2	♡ K J 7 4
◇ 7 4	◇ A 8 3 2
♣ A 5	♣ 7 6

If West opens 1♠, showing a 5-card suit, East ought not to support spades at once. By temporizing with another bid (e.g. 2◇ or a forcing 2NT if available), the superior heart fit can be found. Only 11 tricks are available with spades as trumps, or in no-trumps, but 12 tricks will make if hearts are trumps and hearts are 3-2.

WEST	EAST
♠ K Q 5 2	♠ A J 7 6 3
♡ A Q 7 3	♡ K J 4 2
◇ A 9	◇ 7 3
♣ A 4 3	♣ 6 5

Playing Precision, West opens 1♣ (16+ points) and East responds 1♠, showing five or more spades. It is premature for West to support spades. A rebid of 1NT will allow the heart fit to come to light. 12 tricks can be made in hearts on a 3-2 break. Only 11 tricks are there in spades or no-trumps.

WEST	EAST
♠ K Q 5 3	♠ A 8 7 6 4 2
♡ A 2	♡ 8 4
◇ A J 5	◇ 6
♣ K 10 4 2	♣ A Q J 7

West opens a Precision 1♣ and East replies 1♠. If West supports spades, the best East-West can do is to reach 6♠ or 6NT. If West marks time, say, with 1NT, the club fit can be discovered and a grand slam in clubs would be a fitting reward.

TIP 5:

The Rule of 5: **When the bidding has reached the 5-level in a competitive auction, tend to defend rather than bid on.**

Suppose the bidding has been:

WEST	NORTH	EAST	SOUTH
1♥	1♠	3♥	3♠
4♥	4♠	5♥	No
No	?		

What action should North take?

If you are the weaker side and your sacrifice bidding has pushed the other side to the 5-level, be satisfied with that achievement. Do not sacrifice again. You may be able to defeat them at the 5-level when they might have succeeded one level lower. That is your profit for having pushed them one higher.

If you sacrifice again in 5♠ at pairs, they may well double and you may sustain a bigger loss than others who have been doubled in 4♠ or who have beaten 5♥. On the odd occasion, your excessive sacrifice may drive them into a slam which might fluke its way home on a lucky (for them) lie of the cards. At teams, even if 5♠ doubled costs 'only' 500 against their likely 650, you have to be right three times out of four simply to break even.

If you are the stronger side, it is normally better to accept the penalty they are offering by their sacrifice at the 5-level than push on to the 5-level yourself and risk defeat. If you are the stronger side, do not forget to double. At pairs, you need to be pretty confident of success to attempt the 5-level yourself. If you fail at the 5-level you almost certainly have a bottom. If you double them, you are likely to have company and if 5♠ is failing, you have achieved the best possible result in the circumstances. At teams, you need about a 75% degree of confidence to take the push. The more balanced your hand, the less attractive it is to bid on. A singleton or void in their suit, or four worthless cards in their suit (indicating that partner has a shortage) would be a factor in favour of bidding on.

If you are unable to tell which side has the greater strength, definitely defend, but you do not need to double. On many occasions, neither side can succeed at the 5-level and you might well have been beaten at the 4-level.

Tip 3 (defend at the 3-level) and Tip 5 (defend at the 5-level) are summed up by this memory guide:

Defend on odd occasions.

TIP 6:

The Rule of 6: Part 1: A six-card suit is revealed when responder bids 1NT and later follows with a change of suit.

WEST	EAST
1♠	1NT
2♡	3♣...

Responder in these auctions is denying any support or tolerance for opener's suit, around 6-8 points and ... normally a six-card suit. This would be guaranteed when responder's rebid is at the 3-level and is a sound practical approach if responder rebids at the 2-level.

WEST	EAST
1♠	1NT
2◇	2♡...

Responder would pass the second suit with three cards there and give preference to the first suit (now confirmed as a 5-card suit) with doubleton support. Therefore, if responder does not have two cards in opener's first suit and has less than three cards in opener's second suit, responder is highly likely to have a 6-card or longer suit (although a 5-5-2-1 pattern is possible).

The practical result of this is that opener should pass this new suit rebid by responder. To remove responder's suit, opener would need a 6-5 shape and a void in responder's suit, and even then it may be wrong to remove responder's rebid. Neither 2NT nor 3NT should be used as a rescue.

Responder will not hold more than 8 HCP, since with a 6-card suit and 9 HCP, responder would tend to bid the suit at the 2-level and rebid the suit at the 3-level to convey this kind of hand (e.g. 1♡:2♣, 2◇:3♣).

When opener rebids the same suit (e.g. 1♠:1NT, 2♠ or 1♡:1NT, 2♡) opener is expected to hold a 6-card suit and, therefore, responder will normally pass. Where responder has scanty support for opener's suit and has a long suit, should responder pass opener's major or remove to the long suit at the 3-level? A good guide here is:

The Rule of 6: Part 2: Where opener rebids 2-of-the-suit opened after a 1NT response (e.g. 1♠: 1NT, 2♠ ...) responder subtracts the number of cards held in opener's suit from the number of cards in responder's long suit. If the answer is *below* 6, pass. If the answer is *6 or more*, bid 3 of your long suit.
For example:

Suppose you hold after 1♡:1NT, 2♡...

(1) ♠ K 6	(2) ♠ K 6 5	(3) ♠ 8 7
♡ 7	♡ —	♡ 7
◇ A 8 7 4 3 2	◇ A 8 7 4 3 2	◇ K Q 9 7 6 3 2
♣ 7 6 5 2	♣ 7 6 5 2	♣ J 10 2

(1) Pass. Difference is 5. (6 diamonds minus 1 heart.)
(2) Bid 3◇. Difference of 6. (6 diamonds minus 0 hearts.)
(3) Bid 3◇. Difference of 6. (7 diamonds minus 1 heart.)

TIP 7:

The Rule of 7: **In no-trumps, when intending to hold up with only one stopper in the enemy suit, add the number of cards held by you and dummy in that suit and deduct from 7. The answer is the number of times you must duck.**

Thus, with five cards in the enemy suit, you should duck twice (7−5=2), with 6 cards, duck once and with 7 cards, do not duck at all. This clever rule appeared in *Step By Step Card Play In No-Trumps* by Robert Berthe and Norbert Lebely and is very useful, given that you intend to hold-up anyway:

(1) NORTH	(2) NORTH	(3) NORTH
♠ A Q J 10	♠ A Q J 10	♠ A Q J 2
♡ A 8 4 2	♡ A 4 3	♡ 9 8 3
◇ 10 6	◇ 10 6 2	◇ 10 6
♣ 7 4 3	♣ 7 4 3	♣ Q J 4 2
SOUTH	SOUTH	SOUTH
♠ K 5 4	♠ K 5 4	♠ 7 5 4
♡ K 9 6	♡ K 9 2	♡ K 5
◇ A 8 3	◇ A 8 3	◇ A 8 3
♣ K Q J 2	♣ K Q J 2	♣ A K 8 7 3

In each case ◇ 5 is led and East plays ◇ K. Plan your play.
(1) The Rule of 7 tells you to duck twice (7−5=2) and there is no reason to do otherwise. Win the ◇ A on the third round and play to set up club winners. If West began with five diamonds and East has the ♣ A, all will be well.

(2) The Rule of 7 tells you to duck once (7−6=1) and in order to make your contract this line is fine. Win the second diamond and then tackle the clubs (spade to dummy's 10, club to your K, and if it wins, spade to the J, club to Q and ♠ K to the A, club towards your J-2). This gives you ten tricks if West began with five diamonds and East has the ♣ A. At pairs, however, it pays to duck twice as no switch is dangerous and if West began with four diamonds and East has the ♣ A, ducking once holds you to nine tricks while ducking twice produces ten. The Rule of 7 telling you to duck once would be correct if you did not hold two stoppers in hearts.

(3) The Rule of 7 says to duck twice but here you must not duck at all, since the danger of a switch to hearts is so great. Win the ◇ A and take the spade finesse as often as necessary. This could fail (compared with holding up twice) if West has five diamonds and East has the ♡ A and the ♠ K, but this is far less of a chance than West simply having the ♠ K.

TIP 8:

The Rule of 8: Part 1: **With eight cards including the ace, king and jack, it is normally best to finesse for the queen on the second round of the suit.**

(1) WEST	EAST	(2) WEST	EAST
A K J 7	6 5 3 2	A K J 7 6	5 3 2

(3) WEST	EAST
A K J 7 6 5	3 2

In each of these examples West should cash the ace (in case the queen is singleton), cross to East and lead low to the jack on the second round.

If the lead is with East *and there are no further entries* it is better to take a first-round finesse of the jack than to play the A-K and hope the queen drops.

If West's 7 were replaced by the 10, the same play would be correct in (1) and (2), but in (3), if East has enough entries, it is superior to cross to East at once, take a first-round finesse, cross back to East and finesse again. The reason is that this allows you to finesse twice, while if you cash the ace first, East has only one card left and you can finesse only once. If the suit breaks 3-2 whether you finesse on the first-round or second-round is immaterial, but if the suit is 4-1, the chance of Q-x-x-x with South is 4 times greater than the chance of Q-singleton with North.

The Rule of 8: Part 2: **With eight cards, including the king, queen and ten, it is normally best to finesse for the jack on the second round of the suit.**

(4) WEST	EAST	(5) WEST	EAST
K 7 4 3	Q 10 5 2	K Q 10 2	7 5 4 3

(6) WEST	EAST
K Q 7 3	10 5 4 2

In each of these cases, it is best to lead low from East to West's king. If that wins, then in

(4) lead low to East's 10 next.
(5) cross to East and lead low to West's 10 next.
(6) cross to East and lead low to West's queen next.

Since the ten in (6) is not part of a tenace there is no finesse of the ten available if you do not hold the 9 as well. If East in (6) held 10 9 4 2, then after the king wins cross to East and lead the 10, letting it run if South plays low.

The above guidelines refer only to the correct handling of one suit. There may be many other considerations for the correct management of the complete hand.

TIP 9:

The Rule of 9: Part 1: **With 9 cards including the ace, king and jack, it is normally better to play the two top honours and hope the queen falls than to finesse the jack on the second round.**

(1) WEST	EAST	(2) WEST	EAST
A K J 9 4	7 5 3 2	A 6 5 4 2	K J 9 3

(3) WEST	EAST
A 10 8 4 2	K J 6 3

(1) Play the ace first. If all follow, continue with the king.

(2) Play the ace first. If all follow, play to the king next. Do not play to the king first—cashing the ace allows you to avoid any loser if North began with Q-10-8-7 by virtue of East's jack and nine. If South has Q-10-8-7, two tricks will be lost regardless.

(3) Play to the king first. This has the advantage that if South began with Q-9-7-5, you can avoid losing any trick because of West's ten and eight. If North began with Q-9-7-5, one trick would have to be lost.

You may dispense with the Rule of 9 when there are overriding considerations:

WEST	EAST	
♠ K J 10 4	♠ A 9 6 3 2	West is in a contract of 6♠ and
♡ K 10 3	♡ A Q 5 4	the lead is the ◇ 3. How should
◇ K J 6 4	◇ A	West plan the play?
♣ A Q	♣ 8 5 3	

One line would be to win the lead and play ♠ A and ♠ K. If the ♠ Q does not drop and South has the ♠ Q, tackle the hearts. ♡ K, then ♡ 3 to the ace. If the ♡ J has dropped, cash the 10, ruff a diamond and discard ♣ Q on the ♡ Q. If the ♡ J has not dropped, play the ♡ Q. If the hearts are not 3-3, ruff the heart, play ◇ K and ruff a diamond, hoping to drop the queen. If still no success, try the club finesse. With all these chances it would be unlucky for 6♠ to fail.

Despite the excellent chance of success, it is superior to win ◇ A, cash ♠ A and lead a low spade, finessing if South plays low. If the finesse wins, you can play for the overtrick. If the finesse loses to North's Q-x, North is endplayed. A club return would solve that problem, a heart return provides four heart tricks and allows West's club to be discarded while a diamond lead into the K-J enables two of dummy's clubs to disappear.

If South shows out on the second spade, win the ♠ K and lead a third spade to achieve the same endplay.

The Rule of 9: Part 2: **With 9 cards including king, queen and ten, it is normally better to play for the jack to drop than to finesse the 10 on the second round.**

WEST	EAST	Lead low to the K. If that loses to the A, later play the Q and hope the J drops.
Q 10 7 4 2	K 6 5 3	

The Rule of 9: Part 3: **With 9 cards including the ace, king and ten, cash the ace or king first. If the queen or jack drops, play for that honour card to be a singleton.**

WEST	EAST	If West plays the A and North drops Q or J, it is superior to cross to East and finesse the 10
A K 10 4 2	7 6 5 3	

next than to cash the K hoping North's honour to be from Q-J doubleton. You need very strong reasons to play contrary to Part 3.

The question whether it is better to play for the drop or to finesse for any honour card can be solved by the Even Suit Break Test (see Tip 56).

It is important to appreciate that the correct play of a complete hand may entail an approach contrary to the normal techniques of suit management.

TIP 10:

The Rule of 10:   **When contemplating a penalty double of a suit below game, add your expected trump tricks to the number of tricks the opponents are trying to win. If the answer is 10 or more, you have the right number of trump tricks. If the answer is below 10, your double is not sound.**

The most rewarding doubles can occur at the 1-level, 2-level or 3-level if you have the right requirements:

(1) Strength and length in their trump suit.
(2) 20 or more HCP between you and partner.
(3) A misfit with partner's suit.

The length needed in their trump suit is covered by the Rule of 12 (see page 22). The strength needed is covered by the Rule of 10:

Doubles at the 1-level : 10-7 tricks = 3 trump winners needed.
Doubles at the 2-level : 10-8 tricks = 2 trump winners needed.
Doubles at the 3-level : 10-9 tricks = 1 trump winner needed.

How do you assess winners in their suit?

Count each card beyond the fourth as a winner. In the top four cards, assume declarer leads the suit from the top and estimate how many tricks that will give you. These are not sure winners, but potential tricks. For example:

(1) Q-10-6-5-3: Estimate 3 tricks. One for the fifth card and two more if declarer leads out the A K and another.
(2) K-Q-9-6: Estimate 3 tricks. After A and J which you win, you have K-9 left against declarer's 10.
(3) K-Q-7-6: Estimate 2 tricks. After A and J which you win, declarer's 10-9 against your K-7, gives you just one more trick.

WEST	Partner opens 1♠. Next player intervenes. Would
♠ 7	you contemplate a penalty double if right-hand
♡ Q 10 3	opponent bid:
◇ A J 8 6 3	(a) 2♣? (b) 2◇? (c) 2♡?
♣ K 9 5 2	

(a) You should not look for penalties. You have only one potential club trick. 1+8=9.

(b) You should aim for penalties. You have 3 potential diamond tricks, 3+8=11. Your side has over 20 HCP and you have a misfit with partner. If a double by you here would be for penalties, double. If double by you here would be for takeout (if using negative doubles), pass and then pass again if partner produces the expected re-opening takeout double.

(c) Do not look for penalties. You have only one potential heart trick, 1+8=9. Also the length is inadequate for a 2-level penalty double (see the Rule of 12).

TIP 11:

The Rule of 11 (the most widely known rule of card-play): **If the opening lead is the fourth-highest, deduct the card led from 11. The answer is the number of cards higher than the card led held by the other 3 players. Deduct the higher cards in dummy and your hand and you have the number of higher cards in the missing hand.**

The Rule of 11 is useful for a defender:

NORTH		West leads the 7, dummy plays
A J 6	EAST	low. What should East play?
	K 9 3	

11 - 7 = 4. Dummy has two cards higher than the 7 and so does East. That means South has no cards higher than the 7. East can play low or play the 9. East should not play the king, as this makes the A-J into a double stopper and probably 2 tricks. If the 7 is fourth-highest, West began with Q-10-8-7. If the 7 is not fourth-highest, East will probably still make the king later.

The Rule of 11 is useful for declarer:

NORTH	West leads the 7. How should declarer play?
A 9 3	11 - 7 = 4. Dummy has 2 cards higher than the 7, so
SOUTH	play the 9 from dummy. When it wins, South can
Q J 5	make 3 tricks in the suit by leading the Q later. If the 7 is

fourth highest, West began with K-10-8-7 and if South fails to play dummy's 9, South can be restricted to just the two tricks (which was South's original entitlement anyway).

NORTH	West leads the 5—2 from dummy—jack from East.
K 10 7 2	How should South play? 11 - 5 = 6. Dummy plus
SOUTH	declarer hold 5 cards higher than the 5 and so East's
A 8 3	jack is the only card East has above the 5. Win the

ace and (sooner or later) lead the 8 (running it if West plays low). If West covers with the queen, win the king, return to hand and finesse dummy's 7. If the 5 is fourth-highest, West began with Q-9-6-5 and after East has played the jack, East will be unable to beat the 8, 10 or 7.

If you play for a situation indicated by the Rule of 11 and it fails to eventuate, this does not mean the Rule of 11 is faulty. It means the lead was not fourth-highest.

TIP 12:

The Rule of 12: **When contemplating a penalty double below game, add the number of trumps to the number of tricks the opponents are trying to win. If the answer is 12 or more, you have enough trumps to play for penalties. If the answer is below 12, you do not have enough trumps.**

We saw in the Rule of 10 (see page 20) that the requirements for a successful penalty double at a low-level are:

(1) Strength and length in their trump suit.
(2) 20 HCP between you and partner.
(3) A misfit with partner's suit.

The Rule of 12 reveals whether you have sufficient length in their suit.

Doubles at the 1-level : 12-7 tricks = 5 trumps needed.
Doubles at the 2-level : 12-8 tricks = 4 trumps needed.
Doubles at the 3-level : 12-9 tricks = 3 trumps needed.

WEST
♠ A 10 9 7 5 2
♡ A 6
◇ 7 2
♣ K J 4

With both sides vulnerable, West opens 1♠. North doubles, and East redoubles. South bids 2♣. Should West double for penalties?

Applying the Rule of 12, 8 tricks + 3 trumps = 11, not enough for a sound double. West should pass and let partner clarify the redouble. In a national selection tournament, West did double in the above situation. This was the deal:

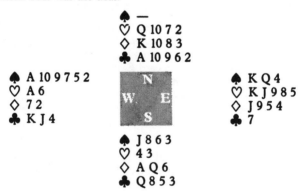

```
                    ♠ —
                    ♡ Q 10 7 2
                    ◇ K 10 8 3
                    ♣ A 10 9 6 2
 ♠ A 10 9 7 5 2                          ♠ K Q 4
 ♡ A 6              N                     ♡ K J 9 8 5
 ◇ 7 2          W.      E                 ◇ J 9 5 4
 ♣ K J 4               S                  ♣ 7
                    ♠ J 8 6 3
                    ♡ 4 3
                    ◇ A Q 6
                    ♣ Q 8 5 3
```

With support for spades, East should have removed the double (4♠ made in the other room), but East clearly expected better clubs with West. Two clubs doubled made with an overtrick.

WEST
♠ 8 6
♡ 9 4 2
♢ Q J 7 6
♣ A K 10 3

With neither side vulnerable, South opens 3♢.
After West and North pass, East doubles, passed by
South. What action should West take?

West can satisfy the Rule of 12 (9 tricks + 4 trumps = 13) and also the
Rule of 10 (9 tricks + 2 trump tricks = 11) and at equal vulnerability,
should certainly pass.

Against 3♢ doubled, West leads ♣K and sees:

```
              ♠ K 10 9 4 2
              ♡ K Q 10 8
              ♢ 5
              ♣ 7 6 5
♠ 8 6              N
♡ 9 4 2        W     E
♢ Q J 7 6          S
♣ A K 10 3
```

East plays a discouraging 2 on the ♣K. What next?

With South likely to hold ♢ A-K and the ♣Q (in view of East's ♣2),
the remaining high cards figure to be with East. You should therefore
switch to ♠8, expecting the complete hand to be something like:

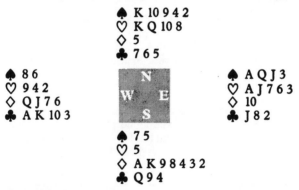

```
              ♠ K 10 9 4 2
              ♡ K Q 10 8
              ♢ 5
              ♣ 7 6 5
♠ 8 6              N            ♠ A Q J 3
♡ 9 4 2        W     E          ♡ A J 7 6 3
♢ Q J 7 6          S            ♢ 10
♣ A K 10 3                      ♣ J 8 2
              ♠ 7 5
              ♡ 5
              ♢ A K 9 8 4 3 2
              ♣ Q 9 4
```

The defence should take 9 tricks and score +1100 at duplicate via:
♣K; ♠8 to the jack; ♣J; third round of clubs won by West; ♠6 won
by East; ♡A; top spade, ruffed by South, overruffed by West;
thirteenth club ruffed with the ♢10 to uppercut declarer. Defence can
be fun!

TIP 13:

The Rule of 13: **If you have a strong trump fit (or a self-sufficient trump suit) and no losers in the first three rounds of any suit, you are likely to win all 13 tricks.**

Corollary: **If you are unable to account for the first three rounds of every suit, be content to try for a sound small slam.**

WEST	
♠ A Q 10 7 6	Suppose partner opened 1♣ and raised your spade response. How should you proceed?
♡ A Q 10	
◇ K Q 5	It requires no more than a check on aces and kings.
♣ K 3	If partner produces two aces and two kings, bid 7NT. If any of those four cards is missing, stop in a small slam.

WEST	
♠ A K 8 3	Suppose partner opened 1♠, how would you
♡ A K 7 5	proceed? Suppose you find partner has the two
◇ K 7	missing aces, what next?
♣ K J 2	Unless your methods are able to establish considerably more, you should be content to bid 6♠

or 6NT. Four aces and four kings yield only eight tricks. It would be a tragedy to bid a grand slam and find partner has ♠J7654 ♡983 ◇AQ ♣AQ3.

Even if partner has ♠QJ7654 ♡J8 ◇AQ ♣A964 the slam odds are only 50% on the club finesse, a poor chance for a grand slam. True, if partner has ♠QJ654 ♡98 ◇AQ3 ♣A5 the grand slam is laydown. That just means that your bidding methods must be sufficiently sophisticated to locate partner's sixth spade and the heart and club shortages.

WEST	
♠ A K Q J 10 7 6	Suppose partner opened 1◇, how would you
♡ A 8	proceed? If you found partner with an ace and three
◇ A 4 3	kings, you could bid 7NT but what if partner
♣ 6	showed an ace and two kings, could you bid a grand slam?

The grand slam could be a poor bet opposite a hand such as ♠53 ♡Q73 ◇K9762 ♣AK5 or it could be laydown opposite ♠53 ♡973 ◇KQ762 ♣AK5.

Modern partnerships use variations of key-card Blackwood to locate not only the aces and kings but also the trump honours.

On the above hand, using 4NT at once over the 1◇ opening enables you to locate the ◇Q. On the first hand partner replies 5♡ (2 key cards, no ◇Q) and shows only one extra king in reply to 5NT, thus enabling you to stop in 6NT. On the second hand, partner replies 5♠ (2 key cards plus the ◇Q) and when one extra king is shown in reply to 5NT (the trump king is not shown twice), you can bid 7NT with absolute confidence.

TIP 14:

The Rule of 30:   **When partner reveals a void and you have a strong trump fit, there are only 30 relevant points, not 40. A small slam can be bid on around 23-24 points, while a grand slam is feasible around the 26 point mark.**

♠ A Q 7	Suppose you open 1♡ and partner bids 3♠ which
♡ K Q 7 6 4	is a splinter promising 4 or more hearts, enough for
◇ 8 4 3	game, and a void in an undisclosed suit. When you
♣ A 4	bid 3NT to ask for the void, partner bids 4◇ to
	show a void in diamonds. What now?

Things could not be more favourable. You should bid 4NT and if you hear 5◇, check for kings with 5NT. If partner reveals two kings, bid 7♡, since you are able to satisfy the Rule of 13: no losers in the first three rounds of any suit. The ♠K and ♣K cover those suits, partner's ♡A with your K-Q covers the trumps and partner's disclosed void in diamonds takes care of those losers. If partner holds ♠K862 ♡A8532 ◇— ♣K952 you would be thrilled to reach 7♡.

On the other hand, if you hold considerable strength opposite partner's void and no significant extra strength in the other suits, you should not venture towards a slam. Suppose that partner's void was in spades. Now your A-Q are wasted values and the duplication (wasted high cards opposite a known shortage) should make you sign off in game. Partner can bid beyond game if partner has significant extra strength.

If the two hands are:

WEST	EAST	
♠ A Q 7	♠ —	You will be very pleased to be no
♡ K Q 7 6 4	♡ A 8 5 3 2	higher than 4♡. Even 5♡ could
◇ 8 4 3	◇ K J 6 2	fail if North leads a singleton
♣ A 4	♣ K 9 5 2	diamond or a rag doubleton
		diamond.

However, if the hands are:

WEST	EAST	
♠ A Q 7	♠ —	It is East who should not be
♡ K Q 7 6 4	♡ A 8 5 3 2	content with merely 4♡. East
◇ 8 4 3	◇ K Q J 6	should figure a small slam to be a
♣ A 4	♣ K Q 5 3	good bet unless two key cards are
		missing. If West has signed off in
		4♡ after learning of the spade

void, East should ask with 4NT and West should show key cards *but excluding the spade control since that is East's void.*

TIP 15:

The Rule of 40: **There are exactly 40 HCP in the pack. When dummy appears, count dummy's points and add your own (and any shown on lead) and any revealed in the bidding. When you deduct this from 40 you will have a good idea where the missing points are likely to be.**

WEST	EAST	WEST	NORTH	EAST	SOUTH
♠ A K 8 6 5 2	♠ 9 7 3			No	No
♡ 6 3 2	♡ 8 5 4	2♠	No	No	No
◇ J 6 2	◇ A 5 3				
♣ 8	♣ A Q J 2	Both sides vulnerable, playing pairs.			

North leads the ♡ J against 2♠. South wins the queen, king and ace of hearts and switches to the ◇ 10. How do you plan the play?

You should *play low* and win the ◇ A. When you play the ♠ A and ♠ K, trumps turn out to be 2-2. South holding Q-10 doubleton. What precautions have you taken and how do you proceed? Do you chance the club finesse for an overtrick?

The precautions you should have taken are (a) not to play the ◇ J on the 10 and (b) to play the ♠ 9 on the first or second round of spades to unblock the suit.

You began with 8 points, dummy with 11 and South has revealed 11 (♠ Q 10 and ♡ A K Q). The remaining 10 points must be with North as South failed to open and has already shown 11 points. You can safely take the club finesse and score an overtrick, but should you be satisfied with that?

As North is marked with ◇ K-Q and ♣ K, you are able to squeeze North (and that is why you did not play your ◇ J on the ten). Run your spades to lead to this ending:

```
                    ◇ K Q
                    ♣ K 9 5

  ♠ 5 2
  ◇ J 6                              ◇ 5
  ♣ 8                                ♣ A Q J 2

              Immaterial
```

Lead the ♠ 5 and the ♠ 2. If North lets go both diamonds, take your ◇ J and the club finesse. If North lets go one diamond and one club, finesse the club, cash the ♣ A dropping the K and cash dummy's last club. Making ten tricks.

If North lets go the ◇ K or ◇ Q on your ♠ 5 at trick 9, do not play a low diamond next to knock out a diamond and set up your jack. A cunning North might have discarded down to ◇ K 7, ♣ K 9. It is safe and certain to play off your last spade first—and then chide partner for not bidding the game! (See also Tips 62 and 63.)

TIPS 16–25: Constructive Bidding

TIP 16:

You know it—you go it

When you become aware of the correct contract, bid it straight away. Do not take partner—and the opponents—on a scenic tour to see all the wonders of your hand when the final destination is known.

Naturally it is necessary to give partner information when you are not yet certain of the correct contract. However, once you do know what's best, go straight to it.

Failing to heed this advice cost in the following situation. Suppose partner opens 1◇, you respond 1♡ and partner rebids 2◇. What action do you take next with:

♠ A Q 9 2   ♡ K Q 6 4   ◇ 7   ♣ A 6 5 4?

This was the complete deal:

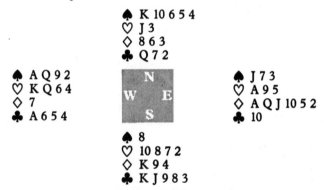

```
                    ♠ K 10 6 5 4
                    ♡ J 3
                    ◇ 8 6 3
                    ♣ Q 7 2
     ♠ A Q 9 2                        ♠ J 7 3
     ♡ K Q 6 4          N             ♡ A 9 5
     ◇ 7            W        E         ◇ A Q J 10 5 2
     ♣ A 6 5 4          S             ♣ 10
                    ♠ 8
                    ♡ 10 8 7 2
                    ◇ K 9 4
                    ♣ K J 9 8 3
```

In a teams match, one West rebid a sensible 3NT over 2◇. Knowing that East would not have four cards in either major, 3NT was the normal spot. North led a natural fourth-highest spade won by West who took the diamond finesse losing to South. The switch to clubs came but West made 11 tricks easily.

At the other table, West rebid 2♠ over 2◇. East gave preference to 3♡ and, belatedly, West bid 3NT. This was the correct contract but the damage had been done. Warned about West's spade holding, North tried the ♣2 lead. West ducked this and ducked the ♣J continuation by South. On this North carefully played ♣Q to unblock the suit and West won the ♣A on the third round.

However, now when the diamond finesse lost, South had two clubs to cash to defeat the contract by one trick.

TIP 17:

Do not be frightened to bid a weak four-card major at the 1-level, whether you are the opener or responder. There are several reasons:

(a) The correct contract may be in your major suit:

WEST	EAST	WEST	EAST
♠ A 8 7 6	♠ 9 5 4 3	1♡	1♠
♡ A K 7 6 4	♡ 5 3	2♠	No
◇ Q 3	◇ K 5 2		
♣ 8 2	♣ A 7 6 4		

The correct contract for East-West is in spades, easily reached if East responds 1♠. If East in trepidation replies 1NT, West may pass or rebid 2♡, both significantly inferior to 2♠ which should make 8 or 9 tricks.

West is too weak to reverse into 2♠ so that if the partnership is to find the spade fit, it is up to East to do it. A good guide for responder is to *reply 1NT only as a last resort*.

(b) If no-trumps is the correct spot, it is often better for the opener to be declarer rather than the responder.

WEST	EAST
♠ A 3	♠ 7 5 4 2
♡ A Q 3	♡ 8 5 4
◇ K Q J 8	◇ 10 7 3
♣ Q J 5 2	♣ A K 4

The best contract is 3NT played by West but if East responds 1NT, then West will be obliged to raise to 3NT and the heart suit loses the benefit of having the lead coming into the tenace. If West is the declarer, the contract is secure on a heart lead, while if East is declarer a heart lead may be fatal by establishing the hearts before the ◇ A is knocked out. Or if East is able to duck the first heart, the killing spade switch is easy to find.

By contrast, a spade response by East allows West to bid the no-trumps first and even if a spade lead proved fatal, the spade bid may successfully ward off an impending spade lead, as most opponents are reluctant to lead a suit bid by dummy.

The weak hand should not snatch a possible no-trump contract from the stronger hand.

TIP 18:

Repeat a 5-card suit only as a last resort, whether you are the opener or the responder.

One of the worst concepts inflicted on bridgekind was the 'rebiddable suit'. While the idea had merit in indicating when one might rebid a suit, it has been widely misinterpreted so that rebidding a 5-card suit became an obligation. 'Rebiddable' means 'able to be rebid', not 'forced to rebid'. More bidding sins are committed under the excuse 'I had to show you I had five, partner' than in any other single area.

There are two distinct situations here:

1. If your rebid is not forcing, be extremely reluctant to rebid a 5-card suit. Do it only as a last resort and check to make sure that you have not overlooked any other option. Suppose you hold:

♠ 76 ♡ A 8 7 6 3 ◇ K 8 4 ♣ 9 7 3

Suppose partner has opened 1♣ and you responded 1♡. What is your rebid if partner rebids (a) 1♠? (b) 2◇?

Suppose partner has opened 1◇ and you responded 1♡. What is your rebid if partner rebids (c) 2♣? (d) 1♠?

(a) Rebid 1NT. The 5-3-3-2 shape is balanced and there is no reason to expect hearts to be a better spot.
(b) Rebid 3♣, giving preference to partner's first suit. As opener has reversed, opener's first suit should be longer than the second. Clubs is a known trump fit, hearts an unknown quantity.
(c) Rebid 2◇, giving preference to opener's first suit. Again, the known fit is in diamonds. The heart situation is unknown.
(d) Rebid 1NT or give preference to 2◇ rather than rebid hearts.

2. If you are in a game-forcing situation, you may rebid your 5-card suit freely below game when you are in doubt as to the correct trump suit. Even here, however, use your discretion and choose some other descriptive bid if possible. If the bidding has commenced 1◇:1♠, 2NT by all means rebid 3♠ on a 5-card suit to check out the best game contract. However, in the same auction, if you have 5 spades and 4 hearts, you must rebid 3♡, not 3♠, so that the best game contract, which may be in hearts, is located.

TIP 19:

Be prepared to rescue partner once, but not twice.

When you are searching for a decent part-score, you often have little space in which to manoeuvre because your strength is quite limited and you want to bail out as soon as possible. Suppose you hold:

♠ 6 4   ♡ 5   ◇ A Q 8 7 6   ♣ A K 4 3 2

and the bidding has been:

You	Partner
1◇	1♠
2♣	2♠
?	

What would you do now?

Partner will normally have a 6-card suit for this sequence (although a powerful 5-card suit is feasible) and you should pass.

Suppose partner's suit had been hearts. Would you also pass 2♡? On the hand given, your best shot is to pass 2♡ because your values in the minor suits will take tricks also in a heart contract and your cards figure to be more useful to partner in hearts than partner's values will be to you in a minor suit contract. In addition, there is a benefit in staying at the 2-level, so that if the decision is close, prefer not to push on to three.

However, suppose that you held:

♠ —   ♡ 5 3 2   ◇ A Q 8 7 6   ♣ A K 4 3 2

and the bidding has been as above. What now over 2♠?

While you are permitted to pass, it is not appealing with a void and a rebid of 3♣ is indicated. Partner is expected to pass or correct to 3◇, but if partner persists with 3♠, you must pass. Under no circumstances should you try 3NT (even if you happened to have a stopper in hearts). Firstly, you have warned partner by your retreat to 3♣ that you have no tolerance for spades (you would have definitely passed with a doubleton and perhaps even with a singleton). Secondly, if 3♠ is a disaster, you hope it will be a salutary lesson and partner will be wiser for the future.

There are many similar situations and you should normally pass after each of these sequences:

(1)	You	Partner	(2)	You	Partner	(3)	You	Partner
	1♠	2♣		No	1NT		No	1♡
	2♠	2NT		2♠	2NT		1NT	2♡
	3♠	3NT		?			3♣	3♡
	?						?	

TIP 20:

When you have a choice of two trump suits, prefer to play in the trump suit of the weaker hand and have the stronger hand as dummy.

Under normal circumstances, it is more attractive to have the stronger hand as declarer and the weaker hand as dummy, but the overriding consideration is to be in the correct contract. Being in the best spot comes first, having the stronger hand as declarer is not nearly as important. Of course, if you can combine being in the right spot and having the opening lead come up to the strong hand, so much the better.

In auctions where the partners seem to be 'fighting' about the trump suit, the stronger hand should give way. The reason is that the stronger hand will almost always be more useful with side tricks to the weaker hand than the weaker hand would be to the stronger. The stronger hand produces the top tricks, the weaker hand produces the trump tricks. Often the weaker hand might produce no tricks if the hand is played in the strong hand's trump suit. Take these hands for example:

WEST	EAST	WEST	EAST
♠ A Q 7 6 5 4	♠ 3	1♠	1NT
♡ 3	♡ Q J 10 9 6 5	2♣	2♡
◇ Q 10	◇ 9 8 6 4	?	
♣ K Q 9 2	♣ A 5		

What action should West take?

Seeing both hands, it is not too tough to pass. At the table, it is not always so easy to 'see', and it is tempting to rebid 2♠.

West should pass. Firstly because West should figure that, as East has at least six hearts and a misfit with spades (see Rule of 6), spades figure to be a worse trump suit than hearts, or at the best, about equal. Secondly, if the decision is at all close, the tip is to play in the trump suit of the weaker hand.

If spades are trumps, the East hand is worth one sure trick and a likely second trick via a club ruff. However, if hearts are trumps, the East hand is worth five tricks, four in hearts plus the ace of clubs. West might make 2♠ if the trump losers can be held to two, but that is no certainty. 2♡, on the other hand, is almost a sure thing: it is hard to see East not making one spade, four hearts and three clubs.

TIP 21:

When the bulk of your high card strength is in your short suits, or is opposite partner's known short suit, prefer to play in no-trumps.

Suppose the bidding has been 1♣ by you, 1♠ by partner. What is your rebid on each of these hands?

(1) ♠ A Q	(2) ♠ 7 2	(3) ♠ 8
♡ J 8 7 2	♡ A J 8 2	♡ A Q J
◇ K J	◇ 7 3	◇ K Q J 8
♣ Q 9 7 4 3	♣ A K 9 6 4	♣ 8 7 6 4 3

1. Rebid 1NT rather than 2♣ on such a rotten suit, 10 of your 13 points are in your short suits. If you use a weak 1NT, you need to foresee the problem and open with 1NT rather than 1♣.

2. Rebid 2♣. Your long suit is strong, your short suits are pathetic, indicating preference for a trump contract.

3. Rebid 1NT, despite the singleton, rather than 2♣ on such a feeble suit. If you use the weak 1NT (where a 1NT rebid would indicate 15-16 points), you must foresee the problem and open 1◇, intending to rebid 2♣ over 1♠.

Suppose you hold:

♠ J 8 7 6 4   ♡ A K J   ◇ 7 3   ♣ J 4 2

You	*Partner*	What now?
	1◇	
1♠	2♣	With so much high card strength opposite partner's
2NT	3♠	singleton or void in hearts, 3NT is likely to be a better
?		shot than 4♠, despite the 8-card trump fit. Suppose
		partner held:

♠ Q 5 3   ♡ 6   ◇ A K J 10 5   ♣ K Q 9 6

Partner has bid the hand well, but 4♠ would be lucky to succeed while 3NT should be easy, and on a heart lead you have good chances for 10 tricks in no-trumps.

Suppose you opened with 1◇ on:

♠ A Q J   ♡ 7 5 3 2   ◇ A 9 8 4 3   ♣ J

and partner responded 3♠, which you are using as a splinter, showing a singleton or void in spades plus support for diamonds and fewer than four cards in hearts. What now?

Applying Tip 21, with excess strength opposite a short suit, you will prefer 3NT to a diamond game, vital if partner holds something like:

♠ 4   ♡ Q J 4   ◇ K Q 7 6 2   ♣ K Q 7 5

Even if partner held the ace of clubs, 5◇ might be defeated by a heart ruff, while 3NT is child's play.

TIP 22:

When the bidding has revealed that the opponents clearly have enough for game or a slam and that you have an excellent trump fit, be quick to make a psychic bid in order to mislead the opponents as to the location of strength and perhaps cause them to miss their game or slam.

Suppose partner opens 2♠ (weak two, 6-card suit, 6-10 HCP) and you hold: ♠ K8752, ♡87, ◇4, ♣Q9542.

What action should you take if second player passes?

The opponents have at least 25 HCP and probably more. As one does not open a weak two with four cards in the other major, the opponents hold at least eight hearts, and as partner will not hold five diamonds, they also hold eight or more diamonds. The opposition have the trump fit and high card values to make at least a game and a slam for them is quite likely. Your side has at best one spade trick in defence (and there is a 50% chance that one opponent is void in spades), while you have no reasonable prospects for a defensive trick and partner may or may not have a trick outside spades.

How can you put this knowledge to your advantage before the opponents locate their fit and strength? Certainly you must take some action and the very least you can do is to bid 4♠ (which is likely to fail but will be a cheap sacrifice). Against naive opponents, 4NT Blackwood may silence them even though you subside in 5♠, after discovering that partner does not have enough aces for a slam! Except at unfavourable vulnerability, 5♠ doubled should be a cheaper result than their game or slam.

Against sophisticated opposition, it is better to try a more subtle approach such as a 2NT response which is used to initiate game or slam auctions, but is invariably based on a strong hand. The drawback to 2NT is that it allows fourth player a cheap entry into the auction at the 3-level.

If you are prepared to be downright brazen, try a bid of 3♡, played as natural, strong and forcing over a weak two. If fourth player doubles this, is it for takeout or penalties? Most partnerships will not have defined the situation. If doubled, you can retreat to 3NT first and ultimately to 4♠.   `

Another neat move if you are not vulnerable and they are vulnerable would be a bid of 4♡, played as a natural sign-off. If everybody passes, you can afford to go ten off undoubled and still show a profit. If doubled, you can hightail it back to 4♠. They may find their game, but miss their slam.

TIP 23:

The concept of a 'reverse bid' ceases to apply if the bidding has progressed beyond two of opener's suit before the opener has had a chance to rebid.

The 'reverse' is a standard part of all natural systems. Opener makes a reverse bid by bidding a new suit at the 2-level which is higher-ranking than the suit opened, such as 1♣:1♠, 2♡. The reverse promises a better-than-minimum opening, normally around 16 points or better, and two suits of unequal length, the first bid suit being the longer.

HAND A	HAND B	HAND C
♠ 3 2	♠ 3	♠ 3 2
♡ A J 5 4	♡ A J 5 4	♡ A J 5 4
◇ 3 2	◇ A 3 2	◇ A Q 3
♣ A K J 4 2	♣ A K J 4 2	♣ A K J 4

In each case the bidding has begun 1♣ by you and 1♠ from partner. What is your rebid?

With A. rebid 2♣—the shape is right for a reverse but the hand is too weak to reverse with 2♡. With B, rebid 2♡—the shape and strength is right for the reverse. With C, rebid with a jump in no-trumps—do not reverse with a balanced hand or where your two suits are of equal length.

Where the bidding starts at a low level, the theory of the reverse will work for unbalanced shapes, since opener can fall back on a rebid of the suit opened with a minimum hand. However, if the bidding has already progressed beyond two of opener's suit there is no convenient minimum rebid and a rebid at the 2-level under these circumstances does not promise extra strength or extra shape. For example:

♠ A J 7 3   ♡ K Q 4 2   ◇ 6   ♣ K 8 4 3

If you opened 1♣ and partner responded with a jump-shift to 2◇, you should rebid 2♡. This does not count as a reverse. The bidding is taken to be the same as though it had started with 1♣:1◇ when you would have rebid 1♡. Your 2♡ rebid now is taken to have the same meaning as the 1♡ rebid over 1◇.

♠ 7 3 2   ♡ A Q 8 6   ◇ A   ♣ K 7 5 4 2

If you opened 1♣, second player overcalled 1♠ and partner bid 2◇, passed to you, what is your rebid?

It would be foolish to forgo a natural 2♡ rebid for fear that you are promising the strength to make a reverse. As the bidding has already bypassed 2♣, the 2-level rebid of your suit, you may rebid 2♡ and partner should not take it as a 'reverse'.

TIP 24:

You may bid a fake suit if (1) partner is known not to hold 4-card support, *or* (2) you have a safe haven if partner does happen to raise the fake suit.

1. *Partner cannot hold support*:

```
♠ A K 7      You  Partner
♡ K 8 4 3          1♢
♢ J 6 2      1♡   3♢
♣ 8 4 3      ?
```

Bid 3♠. Partner's 3♢ denies a 4-card spade holding, so that partner cannot raise to 4♠. 3♠ shows values in spades and focusses partner's attention on the club suit: if partner has clubs stopped, partner can bid 3NT, such as:

$$♠ 65 \quad ♡ A2 \quad ♢ A Q 9 8 7 3 \quad ♣ A Q 2$$

If partner has no values in clubs, you can avoid a silly 3NT, such as:

$$♠ Q 4 2 \quad ♡ A 7 \quad ♢ A K Q 10 7 4 \quad ♣ J 2$$

opposite. Here 5♢ is sound and while 3NT might make, it is a poor gamble.

Similar situations occur frequently:

```
(a) Partner You  (b) Partner You  (c) Partner You  (d) Partner You
    1♣      1♢       1♢      1♡       1♢      1♡       1♣      1♡
    2♣      ?        2♢      ?        2♣      ?        2♢      ?
```

In each of these auctions it is safe for you to bid 2♠ without a 4-card suit, as partner's rebid of 2♣ or 2♢ has denied holding four spades.

Where only two suits have been bid (examples (a) and (b) above), a new suit bid, if fake, shows strength in the suit bid. For example, you would bid 2♠ in auction (a) with ♠ A J 10 ♡742 ♢ A K 972 ♣32 to highlight the need for heart values for no-trumps: and likewise you would bid 2♠ in auction (b) with ♠A2 ♡Q J 106 ♢A Q 62 ♣743.

Where three suits have been bid (examples (c) and (d) above) bidding the fourth-suit tends to deny values in that suit and *asks* for a stopper in that suit for no-trumps. This is logical since if three suits have been bid and you are interested in no-trumps, you would bid no-trumps yourself with the fourth-suit covered. For example, you would bid 2♠ in auctions (c) and (d) with something like ♠732 ♡A Q 98 ♢K Q 6 ♣Q73. If partner has spades covered, 3NT will be sensible: if partner is weak in spades, it will be preferable to play in partner's longer minor, the one bid first.

2. *Partner might hold support*:

Here it is risky to bid a fake suit since you have to be prepared to deal with the contingency that partner raises this fake suit. If you are able to cope with that problem, by all means go ahead and bid your fake suit. Suppose the bidding has been:

Partner You
1◇   1♠
2◇   ?

and you hold:

♠ K J 9 8 2   ♡ A K   ◇ J 9 3 2   ♣ J 2

What action do you take?

The hand is too strong for 3◇, the club suit is too weak for no-trumps. The intelligent move is 2♡, which implies five spades (as well as four hearts). If partner has three spades, partner will bid 2♠ or 3♠: without spade support, partner may bid 2NT with clubs covered and you would raise to 3NT (for example with ♠Q ♡832 ◇AK10764 ♣A103).

However, partner might raise hearts since partner could hold five or six diamonds, but not be strong enough to reverse, e.g. ♠5 ♡J862 ◇AK10764 ♣KQ. If the worst happens and partner bids 4♡, you will need to revert to 5◇ and hope for the best.

If partner raises only to 3♡, you can then try 3♠, hoping partner gets the message that the problem is the club position for no-trumps. If partner perseveres with 4♡, you can again revert to 5◇ and pray.

TIP 25:

With a 6–5 pattern in touching suits, bid the higher-ranking suit first if the suits are weak and you are minimum in high card points, whether you are opener or responder.

With a 6–5 pattern, the normal rule is to bid the longer suit first and then bid then shorter suit twice. The above Tip is to bid the higher ranking suit first, *even if it is the shorter suit*, with poor suits and a minimum hand. A poor suit has two or three losers (headed by at most one of the top three honours), while a strong suit has one or no losers (headed by two top honours or by A-K-Q) preferably with the jack or ten as well.

Examples for opener:

♠ A Q 7 6 4   ♡ J 8 6 4 3 2   ◇ —   ♣ K Q

Weak long suit, minimum high card content. Open 1♠ rather than 1♡. If partner fails to support, bid hearts and then rebid hearts.

♠ A Q J 7 6   ♡ K Q 10 8 4 3   ◇ —   ♣ 7 2

Minimum high card content, but excellent suits. Open 1♡, and if hearts are not supported, bid spades twice. After 1♡:2◇, say, you can rebid 2♠ as a reverse despite only 12 HCP, since the hand has only four losers.

Examples for responder:

♠ Q 2   ♡ Q J 7 4 2   ◇ Q 8 7 6 3 2   ♣ —

If partner opens 1♣ respond 1♡ rather than 1◇. Your suits are poor and the point count is minimum. If partner rebids 2♣, you can rebid 2◇ (confirming five hearts) and then bid 3◇ over 2♠ or 2NT. This is cheaper than bidding 1◇ and then rebidding 2♡ and 3♡ to show the shape, since over 3♡ partner would have to bid 4◇ with diamond preference.

♠ A 2   ♡ Q J 7 4 2   ◇ K J 8 6 4 3   ♣ —

Over 1♣, respond 1◇. Your hand is strong enough to respond 1◇, then bid 2♡ and rebid 3♡, even if partner has not shown support yet.

TIPS 26–35: Competitive bidding

TIP 26:

When contemplating an overcall, apply the suit quality test to check whether the suit itself is adequate.

A suit overcall should be based on a long, strong suit, partly so that it is a sound, lead-directing bid and partly to minimise the risk of incurring penalties. Penalties at low levels are rare, but if your overcalls are solid, they will be much rarer still. It is almost always wrong to make an immediate overcall on a suit like J-x-x-x-x or 10-x-x-x-x

How strong should an overcall be? At the 1-level, the high-card content should be 8-up, at the 2-level 10-up and at the 3-level 12-up. Another good guide is 8 losers or better at the 1-level, 7 losers or better at the 2-level and 6 losers or better at the 3-level. In addition, the suit should be able to pass the SUIT QUALITY TEST: The number of tricks bid should not exceed Length in Suit + Honours in Suit Bid.

Thus for a 1-level overcall, length + honours should be 7 or more: for a 2-level overcall, the total should be 8 or more. If the suit quality is inadequate, then you should pass or double or overcall 1NT, but do not overcall in your suit. You may pass and make a delayed overcall in your suit on the next round if the quality is inadequate for an immediate overcall.

In assessing the honours in your long suit, count the jack and ten as a full value only if supported by a higher honour.

Examples:

GROUP 1:

SUIT	SUIT QUALITY
Jxxxxx	5
Qxxxx	6
Kxxxx	6
Axxxx	6
AKxx	6

Do not overcall in such suits.

GROUP 2:

SUIT	SUIT QUALITY
AKQx	7
AKJx	7
QJxxx	7
AQxxx	7
Kxxxxx	7

Overcall in these suits at the 1-level, but not the 2-level.

GROUP 3:

SUIT	SUIT QUALITY
AKJxx	8
KQJxx	8
KQxxxx	8
QJxxxx	8

Overcall in these suits at the 1-level or 2-level.

GROUP 4:

SUIT	SUIT QUALITY
AKQJx	9
KQJ10x	9
AKJxxx	9
KQ10xxx	9

Overcall in these suits at the 1-level or 2-level or 3-level.

Whether to double or whether to overcall may depend on how the bidding has developed.

Suppose you hold as South:

♠ A K Q 8   ♡ K 7   ◇ J 8 7 4 3   ♣ 6 2

If the bidding has been:

WEST	NORTH	EAST	SOUTH
1♣	No	1♡	?

Your best action is to double as you have both unbid suits.

If the bidding has been:

WEST	NORTH	EAST	SOUTH
1♣	No	1◇	?

Your best move is to call 1♠, as the double is likely to attract an unwelcome heart bid (or lead) from partner, while 1♠ may shut out the opponents' heart suit and indicate the best lead to partner.

If you hold:

♠ Q 7 3   ♡ A J 6 3 2   ◇ K J   ♣ 6 5 4

and right-hand opponent begins with 1♣ or 1◇, you may reasonably overcall 1♡. If, however, the opening has been 1♠ your heart suit is inadequate for a 2 level overcall. The suit quality of the hearts is only 7.

If you hold as South:

♠ J 8 6 4 3   ♡ A K 2   ◇ A 7 6   ♣ Q 5

and right-hand opponent opened, you should not overcall 1♠. The suit is far too weak (suit quality=5). Over a 1♣ opening you can sensibly double, while over 1◇ or 1♡ (or 1♠) you should pass, at least for the time being.

If the bidding were to go:

WEST	NORTH	EAST	SOUTH
No	No	1♡	No
2♡	No	No	?

Now South can sensibly make a delayed overcall of 2♠, and partner should recognise that the spade suit must be quite poor, because of the failure to overcall 1♠ at once over 1♡.

If you hold as South:

♠ A 3   ♡ 7 4 2   ◇ 9 2   ♣ A K J 8 6 4

and the bidding went:

WEST	NORTH	EAST	SOUTH
1♡	No	2♡	?

you have a perfectly respectable 3♣ overcall. The suit quality=9 and you have 12 HCP with 6½ losers.

TIP 27:

If partner opens 1NT, and second player intervenes with a natural suit bid, be prepared to bid 3NT with enough points for game and a no-trump type hand, even though you may not have a stopper in their suit.

Suppose partner, North, opens 1NT and next player bids 2♠. What should you call with: ♠ 4 3 2 ♡ A 8 4 ◇ A Q J ♣ Q 10 8 2?

Best is 3NT, trusting partner for at least one stopper in spades.

This tip, used only if partner opened 1NT (not a suit opening), follows logically from normal bidding strategy:

1. East's overcall will not be based on a solid suit like A K Q x x x, since with such a holding East would not bid 2♠ but should pass and defend (or double and defend). A suit overcall over 1NT is normally based on a suit like A Q x x x x, K Q 10 9 x x, K J 10 x x x and the like.

2. Since East will not have a solid suit for the overcall and you have no stopper in their suit, where will the missing cards in their suit be? Almost invariably partner will have them, given that you hold enough values to try for a game.

3. Common agreements after an intervening bid over 1NT are:

- Change of suit is non-forcing e.g. 1NT:(2◇):2♠ or 1NT:(2♠):3♣.
- Jump-bids below game are forcing e.g. 1NT:(2◇):3♠.
- Bidding their suit is equivalent to Stayman e.g. 1NT:(2♠):3♠ would promise 4 hearts.

4. A more scientific and more accurate approach after an overcall is the Lebensohl 2NT Convention:

- 2NT after their overcall requires partner to bid 3♣
- Change of suit at the 2-level is not forcing
- 2NT & change of suit at the 3-level over the 3♣ 'puppet' is not forcing
- Change of suit at the 3-level (without 2NT) is forcing
- 3NT at once over the overcall *denies* a stopper in their suit
- 2NT and then 3NT after the 3♣ puppet *promises* a stopper in their suit
- Bidding their suit at once is Stayman, but *denies* a stopper in their suit
- 2NT followed by bidding their suit after the 3♣ puppet is Stayman but *promises* a stopper in their suit.

TIP 28:

Do not commit yourself to 3NT until you have made sure a major suit game is not feasible.

Suppose partner has opened 1♠. What do you respond with:

♠ Q 7   ♡ A K 6 2   ◇ A J 3   ♣ J 10 8 2? It could be an error to bid 3NT at once. Better to bid 2♣ initially and, if partner does not reveal a heart suit, it is time enough to try 3NT then. Partner could hold: ♠ K J 8 6 5   ♡ Q 9 7 5   ◇ 6   ♣ A Q 3 where 4♡ is very attractive while 3NT could fail.

Likewise, suppose the bidding has been:

WEST	NORTH	EAST	SOUTH
	1◇	Dble	No

How should West plan the bidding with:

♠ Q J 3   ♡ K 7   ◇ Q 9 4 3   ♣ A Q 8 2.

Many would choose a 3NT reply but that could be premature. If partner has five spades, 4♠ would probably be superior. Here are some possible combinations:

(A)
WEST	EAST
♠ Q J 3	♠ A 9 5 4
♡ K 7	♡ A 8 6 2
◇ Q 9 4 3	◇ 6 2
♣ A Q 8 2	♣ K J 5

WEST	NORTH	EAST	SOUTH
	1◇	Dble	No
2◇(1)	No	2♡	No
3NT(2)	No	No	No

(1) Artificial, game force
(2) 2♡ denies holding five spades

(B)
WEST	EAST
♠ Q J 3	♠ K 8 4 2
♡ K 7	♡ A J 6
◇ Q 9 4 3	◇ 8 5
♣ A Q 8 2	♣ K J 9 7

WEST	NORTH	EAST	SOUTH
	1◇	Dble	No
2◇	No	2♠	No
2NT(1)	No	3NT	All pass

(1) East could still have five spades for the 2♠ reply, so West marks time with 2NT.

(C)
WEST	EAST
♠ Q J 3	♠ K 8 6 5 2
♡ K 7	♡ A Q J 4
◇ Q 9 4 3	◇ 6
♣ A Q 8 2	♣ K 4 3

WEST	NORTH	EAST	SOUTH
	1◇	Dble	No
2◇	No	2♠	No
2NT	No	3♡(1)	No
4♠	No	No	No

(1) Confirms four hearts and therefore five spades.

TIP 29:

Do not allow your opponents to play a suit part-score at the two-level unless you have length and strength in their suit. If opponents hold a primary trump fit (they bid and supported a suit) it is almost always wrong to pass it out at the 2-level.

Suppose you hold as West:

♠ A J 7 4 2   ♡ K J 3   ◇ 6   ♣ K Q 8 2

(1)	WEST	NORTH	EAST	SOUTH
	1♠	2◇	No	No
	?			

(2)	WEST	NORTH	EAST	SOUTH
	1♠	2♣	No	No
	?			

(1) Double and ask partner to choose spades, hearts or clubs.
(2) Pass. You have length and strength in their suit.

If the bidding has been:

WEST	NORTH	EAST	SOUTH
1♡	1♠	2♡	2♠
No	No	?	

East should invariably compete to the 3-level. Where both sides have a trump fit and the points are roughly even, both sides can usually make 8 tricks: occasionally one makes 7 and the other 9. It pays you to be consistent and always push to the 3-level in auctions such as these. The possibilities are:

(1) You make your 3-level contract. Obviously better than letting them play.

(2) You are only one off in your 3-level contract. Again better than if they make their contract.

(3) They push to the 3-level above you and fail. Again you are better off.

(4) They push to the 3-level above you and make. You are no worse off than if you had passed it out at the 2-level.

(5) You fail at the 3-level and it costs you more than their contract was worth. This is feasible but rare. Even when vulnerable, it pays you not to sell out at the 2-level. (See also Tip 3.)

TIP 30:

Re-open the bidding with delayed overcall, delayed double or delayed 2NT, if opponents bid and support a suit to the 2-level and then pass.

Where the auction has been something like:

WEST	NORTH	EAST	SOUTH	or	WEST	NORTH	EAST	SOUTH
		1♡	No		1♣	No	1♡	No
2♡	No	No	?		2♡	No	No	?

It is usually wrong for South to pass the bidding out. The opponents have found a trump fit but have not pushed towards a game. They do not have 25-26 points (they would have bid a game) and they probably do not have 23-24 points (one of them would have tried for a game). The points are roughly equal between both sides, and if they have a trump fit, you may have one also. In that case do not sell out at the 2-level (see Tip 29). This advice does not apply to rubber bridge where the 2-level would give the opponents game and where they may have considerable undisclosed strength.

The actions available when you have not entered the bidding earlier are:

1. The Delayed Overcall: This promises a five-card or longer suit but the suit will be poor if you could have overcalled at the 1-level. In the above auctions South should bid 2♠ with:

♠1087643 ♡873 ◇A8 ♣K7
or 3♣ with:
♠8 ♡J743 ◇Q2 ♣KQ9765.

Length in their suit means partner will be short if they hold 8 or 9 cards together.

2. The Delayed Double: This shows support or tolerance for the missing suits. South would double 2♡ with:
♠K864 ♡7 ◇A843 ♣J972.

The double will normally deny the high card values for a normal takeout double, because of the failure to take action on the first round.

3. The Delayed 2NT: This shows support for both minors, at least four cards in each. South would bid 2NT over 2♡ with:
♠62 ♡53 ◇K8742 ♣AJ54.

A delayed 2NT will usually not have a 5-5 or 6-5 pattern because of the failure to use an immediate 'unusual 2NT' overcall.

When partner makes a delayed overcall, double or 2NT, keep the bidding at the cheapest possible level. Partner's failure to take action on the first round signifies weakness and partner's delayed action already takes your strength into account.

TIP 31:

Do not compete for a part-score at the 4-level.

In order to make 4♡ or 4♠, you require 25-26 points. In order to make 4♣ or 4◇, you therefore need the same. If both sides are bidding and you know you do not have the values for game, it is unwise to venture beyond the 3-level. When the points are roughly even and both sides have a trump fit, both sides can usually make 8 tricks, occasionally one side can make 9 tricks, but it is rare for either side to make 10 tricks. Even if the rate of success for a 4-level part-score in such circumstances were one in two (and the success rate is much lower in fact) it would not pay you to venture to the 4-level.

Firstly, you may well go minus when they were going minus. There is a prevalent feeling that the judgment of the opposition is infallible, but they are just as prone to error as you are (or more prone to error if you have the necessary self-confidence). As they are likely to fail at the 3-level, why take that result away from them?

Secondly, there is a far higher incidence of penalty doubles at the 4-level since they know you are bidding beyond your means. While you will frequently escape unscathed with your 2-level and 3-level competitive manoeuvres, this invulnerability does not extend to the 4-level.

The bidding has been:

WEST	NORTH	EAST	SOUTH
1♠	No	2♠	Dble
3♠	?		

What should North do with:
♠873   ♡92   ◇J3   ♣KQ10765?

Answer: Do not compete for a part-score at the 4-level. Pass and lead ♣K.

The bidding has been:

WEST	NORTH	EAST	SOUTH
1♣	No	1♡	No
2♡	No	No	3◇
No	No	3♡	No
No	?		

What should North do with:
♠A3   ♡76   ◇Q854   ♣K7642?

Answer: Pass. Partner's *delayed* overcall has already pushed them one higher. Be grateful partner bid at all.

TIP 32:

If an opponent passes after long consideration—you should probably pass too.

If the bidding has started:

WEST	NORTH	EAST	SOUTH
1♠	No	2♠	No
Pass	?		

Tips 29 and 30 recommend that you dislodge the opposition from the safety of the 2-level—do not sell out at two—and find some delayed action to push them to the 3-level. The essence of successful part-score bidding is to push them from two to three.

However, if West thought for a long time before passing 2♠, North should pass out 2♠ unless the delayed action is absolutely clearcut. The reason for the long trance is obvious: West was very close to inviting game. If North gives the opposition another chance, the auction may well develop like this:

WEST	NORTH	EAST	SOUTH
1♠	No	2♠	No
Pass*	Dble	3♠	No
4♠	No	Pass	No

*After much deliberation

East, picking up the message from West's trance, pushes to 3♠ and West bids one more and now you have to defend a touch-and-go game. If the cards lie a little luckily for them, 4♠ might make and there are few things more annoying than chalking up a game for them when you could have passed it out at two. Save yourself the anguish and let sleeping dogs lie.

It is true that the Laws state that East is not to be influenced by partner's hesitation but you are better off protecting yourself than having a confrontation with East who will claim 'I was super-maximum for my raise . . . did partner really hesitate? . . . Gosh. I didn't even notice that.' etc. etc. Even if you pursue it, there is no guarantee that an Appeals Committee will see it your way. Look after yourself rather than bleat later 'We wuz robbed'.

Another occasion when you should be reluctant to compete is against notorious underbidders. You know better than I do which pairs at your club regularly play in 2♠, making five, and so on. If not, make a note of such results and check the pairs' names after the session. You will gradually build up a list of habitual underbidders against whom you do not need to compete to achieve a good result. Their poor bidding will give you a good result already and if you push, you might just push them into a making game they would not have bid.

TIP 33:

Do not sacrifice on flat hands.

(1) Suppose neither side is vulnerable and the bidding has been:

WEST NORTH EAST SOUTH
3♣ No ?

What action should South take with: ♠864 ♡763 ◊K54 ♣Q762?

(2) What would your answer be if East had doubled 3♣ for takeout?

There is a temptation in each case to bid 5♣ since the opponents are clearly cold for a game. However, South should not bid 5♣ in either auction. If 5♣ is doubled, the cost will certainly be more than their game is worth, the normal consequence of sacrificing on a flat hand. Furthermore, by tipping them off that you have a big club fit, you may push them into a making slam which they might not have been able to reach. *Give partner's pre-empt a chance to work.*

For the first auction the cards might be:

```
              ♠ 9
              ♡ J 9 4
              ◊ 8 7
              ♣ A K 9 8 5 4 3
♠ A Q J 2                      ♠ K 10 7 5 3
♡ A K Q 5                      ♡ 10 8 2
◊ Q J 9 2                      ◊ A 10 6 3
♣ 10                           ♣ J
              ♠ 8 6 4
              ♡ 7 6 3
              ◊ K 5 4
              ♣ Q 7 6 2
```

If the bidding starts 3♣:(Pass):5♣:(Dble), East cannot get it wrong. 5♠ makes and 5♣ doubled is three off. South's best shot is a subtle 4♣. The advantage is that West's double may be less clearly for takeout and -300 is a sound result. Also, slam might be on (interchange the East-West diamonds) but if you pass 3♣, East might jump to 4♠ over 3♣ doubled and fire West into trying for the slam. Over 3♣:(Pass): 4♣: (Dble), East is unlikely to bid 5♠ and 4♠ may be based on no significant values at all.

For the second auction interchange the East-West hands. After 3♣:(Dble):South should pass or again bid just 4♣. Now 5♣ doubled would cost -700 and East-West do have slam available. If the auction bounces 3♣:(Dble):5♣:(5♠), East is likely to bid 6♠.

TIP 34:

Do not double an artificial cue-bid or an artificial bid in a relay system sequence without very good reason.

Where their side has clearly the balance of strength and they embark on a cue-bidding sequence, there is a constant temptation to double a cue-bid with some strength in that suit in order to indicate to partner what to lead. You should almost always resist that desire unless you feel that only that lead from partner will defeat their slam.

The reasons against speculative lead-directing doubles are:

1. If you are strong enough to believe the slam is likely to fail anyway, your double may inhibit them from reaching the failing slam.

2. By revealing where your strength lies, you allow the opponents to value up a singleton holding in that suit and thus reach a contract they otherwise might not have reached.

3. If they have reached cue-bids of second round controls and you double a cue-bid of the king when you hold A-Q. . . . you may drive them into playing a making slam (e.g. 6NT) from the right side rather than a possibly failing slam when partner finds the right lead without your double.

4. Doubles in a cue-bidding auction give the opponents extra space to exchange information.

e.g.:

WEST	NORTH	EAST	SOUTH
1♠	No	3♠	No
4♣	No	4◇	Dble . . .

The double allows West to redouble to show second-round control and pass to deny second-round control. If West passes, East can redouble with second round control or bid anything else without such control. Without South's double, East-West would be much higher before this information could be exchanged.

Likewise, modern relay systems function best with plenty of bidding space. A double in a relay auction gives them more space as it allows two additional actions (Pass & Redouble) and thus saves two steps and gives the relayers more room to move. This is an expensive price if the double is not vital.

TIP 35:

Do not double a suit slam with just two aces and do not double a suit slam with just strong trumps.

Suppose the bidding has been:

WEST	NORTH	EAST	SOUTH
1♡	No	3♣	No
3♡	No	6♡	No
Pass	?		

On which of these hands should North double?

(a) ♠ A J 7 3   (b) ♠ K 5 3
    ♡ 7 2   ♡ Q J 10 9
    ♢ A 8 7 6 2   ♢ 8 7 6 2
    ♣ 6 2   ♣ 9 3

The answer is that North should not double with either hand. On hand (a) unless the opponents are the rawest of beginners, they will have heard of Blackwood and would not jump to slam missing two aces without checking first. Why did they not check? Because they are not worried about two aces. Why not? Because East is staring at a void. For example:

WEST   EAST
♠ K Q   ♠ —
♡ K J 8 6 4 3 ♡ A Q 10 5
♢ Q J 4   ♢ K 9 3
♣ 8 3   ♣ A K 9 7 5 4

If North does double on (a), East might well redouble. Thus, North is risking to lose an extra 590 (6♡+180 v 6♡ redoubled 720+50 for the insult) to gain an extra 50 (or 100 if East-West are vulnerable). North would have to be right 12 times out of 13 (6 out of 7 if E-W vulnerable) just to break even.

On (b), you are certainly defeating 6♡ but that is the only slam you can beat for sure. It would be dumb to double 6♡ and find them running to 6NT which you cannot beat. For example:

WEST   EAST
♠ A 5   ♠ 7
♡ K 8 6 5 3 2 ♡ A 7 4
♢ K Q J   ♢ A 9 5 3
♣ 7 2   ♣ A K Q J 5

East-West are unlucky to reach 6♡ which fails on the 4-0 break. 6NT is better but not easy to judge and 90% of the time 6♡ would be fine. If North does double 6♡ with ♡ Q-J-10-9, either East or West might sniff out the problem and run to 6NT, giving North-South a terrible result instead of a great one.

The moral is that if the opponents have reached a slam which is due to fail you do not need to double to obtain a good score. Not at rubber bridge, nor at duplicate. And if you regularly refrain from doubling their slams with Q-J-10-9 or K-Q-J in trumps, you will gain a reputation for having a generous and magnanimous nature.

TIP 36:

Do lead partner's suit, even though the opponents have bid no-trumps afterwards.

Suppose the bidding has been:

WEST	NORTH	EAST	SOUTH
	1◇	1♡	1NT
No	3NT	All pass	

What should West lead from:

(a) ♠ J 10 7 3 2 (b) ♠ J 10 7 3 2
    ♡ 8 2   ♡ 8 2
    ◇ Q 4   ◇ A K 3
    ♣ 6 5 4 3   ♣ 6 5 4

It is normal to lead partner's suit, but many players strike out elsewhere when partner's overcall is followed by a no-trump bid, indicating at least one stopper in partner's suit. This strategy is short-sighted. While it is true they have a stopper, your function is to eliminate that stopper. If you do not lead partner's suit, they will still have the stopper later. For example:

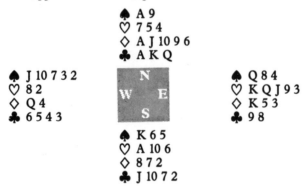

          ♠ A 9
          ♡ 7 5 4
          ◇ A J 10 9 6
          ♣ A K Q

♠ J 10 7 3 2   ♠ Q 8 4
♡ 8 2   ♡ K Q J 9 3
◇ Q 4   ◇ K 5 3
♣ 6 5 4 3   ♣ 9 8

          ♠ K 6 5
          ♡ A 10 6
          ◇ 8 7 2
          ♣ J 10 7 2

After the above auction, a heart lead will defeat 3NT. Any other lead gives declarer at least 10 tricks on normal play.

If partner has a suit like KQJ10x or AQJ10x, declarer will have one stopper. Your lead eliminates that stopper and sets up the rest of partner's suit as winners. If partner's suit is something like KJ10xx or KQ10xx and declarer has AQx or AJx, declarer has two stoppers. Two leads of the suit will be needed to knock out those stoppers, but if you decline to lead partner's good suit those stoppers will still be there.

When should you decline to lead partner's suit after such an auction? If you have a goodish five-card or six-card suit and *entries*, then you may choose your own suit to lead. Even if your suit is good, it will be of little avail to set it up if you have no subsequent entry.

With Hand (b), a spade lead is a sound alternative to the heart, because of your diamond holding. Just as declarer with a choice of suits to attack would choose to set up the long suit in the hand which has the entries, so the defenders must follow the same policy. For example:

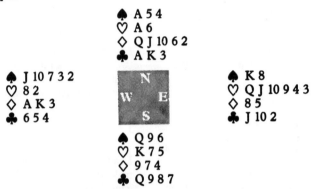

```
                    ♠ A 5 4
                    ♡ A 6
                    ◇ Q J 10 6 2
                    ♣ A K 3
  ♠ J 10 7 3 2            N            ♠ K 8
  ♡ 8 2                              ♡ Q J 10 9 4 3
  ◇ A K 3          W         E        ◇ 8 5
  ♣ 6 5 4                S            ♣ J 10 2
                    ♠ Q 9 6
                    ♡ K 7 5
                    ◇ 9 7 4
                    ♣ Q 9 8 7
```

After the above auction, declarer could and almost certainly would succeed on a heart lead, as East has no easy late entry. On a low spade lead, East will win with the king and as long as a spade comes back, 3NT will be beaten. Even if declarer rises with ♠A at trick one, East can defeat the game by unblocking ♠K.

TIP 37:

From three to an honour in partner's suit, lead the bottom card—do not lead top.

When partner bids a suit, it is normal to lead that suit. The card to lead, however, is the standard card and not an abnormal one. From three to an honour, such as K72, Q83, J75, 1052 the standard lead is the bottom card. To lead top can cost a trick on layouts like these:

(a)   A 5
K 7 2   Q 9 8 4 3
      J 10 6

Lead the king and South has two tricks. Lead low and South has only one.

(c)   8 5
A 4 3   K J 10 9 2
      Q 7 6

Lead the ace and South makes a trick. Lead low and if East wins the king and returns the jack, South makes no trick. (Lead the ace in a suit contract, low in no-trumps.)

(b)   10 2
Q 8 3   A 9 7 6 5
      K J 4

Lead the queen and South has two tricks. Lead low, and if East wins the ace and returns a low card, South has only one trick.

(d)   A 2
J 7 5   Q 9 8 6 4
      K 10 3

Lead the jack and South can make three tricks (win ace and later finesse the ten). Lead low and South can be held to two tricks.

Not only may the top card from honour to three cost a trick, it may also destroy a complete defence. For example:

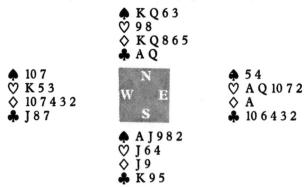

North opens 1♦. East overcalls 1♡ and North-South reach 4♠. If West leads the king of hearts, South can make 4♠ easily.

On the correct *three* of hearts lead, East wins the ace, plays off the ♦A, leads a low heart to West's king (vital as an entry) and ruffs the diamond return for one off.

TIP 38:

From three low cards in partner's suit, lead middle or bottom—do not lead top-of-nothing.

From three rag cards, some lead middle (and follow with the top card —middle-up-down or M.U.D.) while others lead the bottom card. The purpose is to deny a doubleton. With a doubleton, the order of cards is higher-then-lower. With either of the above methods, partner will see lower-then-higher and can deduce therefore that your lead was not a doubleton and that you hold at least one more card in the suit. This information may be critical to the defence:

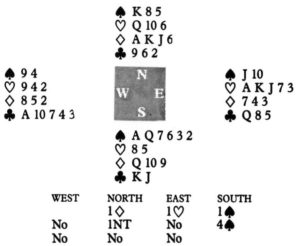

```
                    ♠ K 8 5
                    ♡ Q 10 6
                    ◇ A K J 6
                    ♣ 9 6 2
      ♠ 9 4                              ♠ J 10
      ♡ 9 4 2             N              ♡ A K J 7 3
      ◇ 8 5 2         W       E          ◇ 7 4 3
      ♣ A 10 7 4 3        S              ♣ Q 8 5
                    ♠ A Q 7 6 3 2
                    ♡ 8 5
                    ◇ Q 10 9
                    ♣ K J
```

WEST	NORTH	EAST	SOUTH
	1◇	1♡	1♠
No	1NT	No	4♠
No	No	No	

If West leads the *nine* of hearts, East may try to cash three rounds of hearts, reading West's high-then-low as a doubleton and therefore placing South with three hearts. If West leads low-then-high, East can deduce after the second lead of hearts that South will ruff the third round. With no hope of tricks in the red suits, East should switch to a club.

The correct club is the five—bottom from honour to three. If South misguesses and plays the king (a reasonable misguess as East bid and West did not), the defence can take two clubs to defeat 4♠. If South guesses to play the jack, South succeeds. Without a club switch from East by trick three, the defence has no chance. If East plays a third heart, South ruffs, draws trumps and discards a club on the thirteenth diamond.

Top-of-nothing is less risky in no-trump contracts but it may still mislead partner as to the length held by you and, therefore, by declarer. With this layout at no-trumps:

$$\heartsuit\ 7\ 6$$

$$\heartsuit\ 9\ 4\ 2 \qquad\qquad\qquad \heartsuit\ A\ K\ J\ 5\ 3$$

$$\heartsuit\ Q\ 10\ 8$$

If West leads the nine, East may place South with Q-10-x-x and may elect to win the first lead and switch instead of continuing the suit.

It is safe to lead top-of-nothing when partner knows you cannot hold a doubleton. Suppose in the above layout the bidding had started:

WEST	NORTH	EAST	SOUTH
		1♡	No
2♡	Dble	No	2NT...

Now it would be sensible to lead the *nine* of hearts denying an honour, since West is bound to have at least three hearts for the raise.

TIP 39:

When making an unbid short suit lead in no-trumps, prefer a major to a minor.

There are three situations when you might prefer a short suit lead in no-trumps:

1. Your opponents have shown length in your long suit.
2. Your long suit is hopelessly weak and your hand has no entries.
3. Your long suit is an unattractive four-card suit.

WEST		WEST	NORTH	EAST	SOUTH
♠ 8 4 3				No	1♡
♡ A J 6 4 2		No	2♣	No	2NT
◇ 9 5 2		No	3NT	All pass	
♣ A 2					

West's lead?

Without South's 1♡ bid, a low heart would appeal. It would be foolish to lead a heart into the bidder unless you had a solid sequence. With hearts and clubs excluded, it is a guess between spades or diamonds. However, it is better to choose spades. Opponents are likely to bid any major held, so the absence of a spade bid may indicate partner has the spades. Opponents are less concerned about concealing a minor, so that the absence of a diamond bid does not preclude their having length in diamonds.

WEST		WEST	NORTH	EAST	SOUTH
♠ A J 4 2			No	No	1NT
♡ J 10 3		No	No	No	
◇ J 10 3					
♣ J 4 2					

West's lead?

It is not appealing to lead from a four-card suit with broken honours like A-Q-x-x or A-J-x-x, particularly against a low-level no-trump contract or where declarer opens 2NT, passed out. Such leads are more likely to cost than to gain, and a lead from a decent three-card holding often works out better. Here, the jack of hearts is the best start.

TIP 40:

In no-trumps, if you hold a very weak hand, prefer not to lead a major which partner could conveniently have indicated at the one-level.

Suppose the bidding has been:

WEST	NORTH	EAST	SOUTH
	1♡	No	1NT
No	3NT	All pass	

WEST
♠ 8 7 2
♡ J 9 6 4 3
♢ J 2
♣ 8 7 2

West's lead?

On the basis of Tip 39 (lead a major rather than a minor when making a short suit lead), you would be inclined to lead a spade. However, there are contrary indications on the auction. With your paltry holding, partner almost certainly has the values for a bid, yet partner passed. The failure to overcall 1♠ or to double indicates partner does not have the spade length expected. On this basis, a minor lead is more appealing and prefer the longer to the shorter.

The complete hand might be like this:

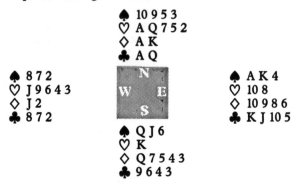

♠ 10 9 5 3
♡ A Q 7 5 2
♢ A K
♣ A Q

♠ 8 7 2
♡ J 9 6 4 3
♢ J 2
♣ 8 7 2

♠ A K 4
♡ 10 8
♢ 10 9 8 6
♣ K J 10 5

♠ Q J 6
♡ K
♢ Q 7 5 4 3
♣ 9 6 4 3

The spade lead helps declarer set up the extra tricks needed while either red suit gives declarer time to unblock the diamonds and lead a spade, again establishing the tricks needed. A club lead sets up five tricks for the defence before declarer can get started.

On other layouts, a diamond lead might be successful, but partner's silence means a spade lead is rarely likely to work in these circumstances.

TIP 41:

Do not lead a suit bid or implied by the opposition.

Whether the contract is no-trumps or trumps, it is rarely worthwhile leading a suit in which an opponent has length, unless you have a solid four-card sequence (such as K-Q-J-10-x or Q-J-10-9-x). The logic is that declarer almost always will have to tackle a long suit to develop the tricks needed and if you lead that suit, you are assisting declarer in that task.

Suppose the opponents bid, without interference, 1♡:2♣, 2♡:4♡. With no attractive lead, many average Wests would lead a club, especially from a doubleton. Some would seek to justify this by referring to the 'Lead-through-strength' rule. With a singleton club and a weak hand, a club lead might be reasonable—otherwise West should choose spades or diamonds. The 'Lead-through-strength' rule does *not* apply to the opening lead *and does not apply to a long suit in dummy*, only a shortish holding (doubleton or tripleton).

WEST		WEST	NORTH	EAST	SOUTH
♠ Q 8 7 4 3		No	No	No	1NT
♡ A 2		No	2♣	No	2♡
◇ 7		No	2NT	No	3NT
♣ Q 8 7 4 3		No	No	No	

West's lead?

On the basis of Tip 39 (major rather than minor), a spade lead would be indicated, but if the opponents had bid 1♡:1♠, 1NT:3NT you would not lead a spade, as the suit had been bid. The above auction is the same *in effect*. North's 2♣ Stayman enquiry and subsequent rejection of hearts implies four spades, so you should reject spades as a disclosed suit and lead a club.

Another common instance when a suit is shown although not bid is when the bidding starts:

WEST	NORTH	EAST	SOUTH
	1◇	No	1NT ...

West should be wary of leading a club since South figures to hold at least four clubs. South should have bid 1♡ or 1♠ with a four-card major and raised diamonds with four-card support. Lacking four cards in spades, hearts and diamonds, South will have four or more clubs and only a strong sequence with West would indicate a club lead. Without that, prefer the stronger major if 1NT is passed out.

TIP 42:

In a trump contract, do not lead from an ace-high suit (unless it is headed by the ace *and* king).

While leading from any honour entails a risk, leading from a suit headed by the ace (without the king) is probably the riskiest lead against a trump contract. (It is all right to lead from such a suit in no-trumps.) The most common outcome of such a lead is that declarer makes more tricks than entitled. Take these layouts:

(1)
```
        8 7 4
A 9 2           J 10 6 5
        K Q 3
```

(2)
```
        10 9 6 3
A 5 4            K Q
        J 8 7 2
```

(3)
```
        7 6 2
A 5 4           Q 10 9 8
        K J 3
```

(4)
```
        K 7 4
A 9 2           J 10 8 5
        Q 6 3
```

In each case, if West leads the ace, South makes two tricks. If West does not lead the suit, South can be held to just one trick.

Given that declarer and dummy have the majority of points, the odds are that you are likely to set up winners for declarer rather than your side. Even ace-doubleton, seeking a ruff, is not likely to work unless you have a very weak hand. Leading from a suit headed by ace-king is not as risky since the first lead has not established any winners for declarer yet, and after seeing dummy and partner's signal you are in an informed position whether to continue or switch.

If you must lead from an ace-high suit, lead the ace, not a low one. Leading low runs the risk of never making the ace at all (for example, if declarer or dummy has K-singleton, if either opponent has a singleton and the other has the king, or if declarer can win the king and later discard the other losers in that suit before you can take your ace).

Instances when you can reasonably run the risk of leading the ace from an ace-high suit are:

1. Against a pre-emptor, who is unlikely to have a vital outside king.
2. When partner is almost certain to be able to ruff the second round of the suit.
3. Against a slam when you have a certain or almost certain second trick.

However, if you *never* lead from an ace-high suit in a trump contract for the rest of your life, you will enjoy far more happiness than regret.

TIP 43:

When dummy has revealed a long suit, lead an unbid suit. Make an attacking lead from a suit with one or more top honours. Do not lead trumps and do not lead from a suit of three or four rags.

Suppose the bidding has been:

WEST		WEST	NORTH	EAST	SOUTH
♠ 6 2		No	1♣	No	1♠
♡ A 8 7 3 2		No	3♣	No	3♠
◇ K 9 7 4		No	4♠	All pass	
♣ 7 2					

West's lead?

Declarer's normal plan when dummy has a long suit is to draw trumps and use the long suit to discard losers. In such cases, it is vital not to lead trumps (this would help declarer) or dummy's long suit (except in desperation, when you have a singleton and a weak hand). The defence tricks will normally come from the unbid suits and it is best to attack one of those, preferably the one in which you have some high cards. It is not likely that partner's hand will be good enough to make a lead from a rag suit useful.

In this case, you have to choose between hearts and diamonds. As you should not lead from a suit headed by the ace (Tip 42), you should select a low diamond. The complete deal:

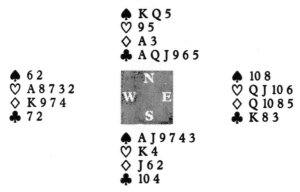

	♠ K Q 5	
	♡ 9 5	
	◇ A 3	
	♣ A Q J 9 6 5	

♠ 6 2		♠ 10 8
♡ A 8 7 3 2		♡ Q J 10 6
◇ K 9 7 4		◇ Q 10 8 5
♣ 7 2		♣ K 8 3

	♠ A J 9 7 4 3	
	♡ K 4	
	◇ J 6 2	
	♣ 10 4	

On the diamond lead, East will obtain the lead sooner or later to push the ♡Q through, giving the defence two hearts, one diamond and a club. A heart lead is the usual disaster, giving declarer the king. On a black suit lead declarer wins, takes two rounds of trumps and then sets up the clubs. The defence never comes to its diamond trick.

TIP 44:

Do not lead a singleton against a trump contract from a very strong hand.

Suppose the bidding has been:

WEST		WEST	NORTH	EAST	SOUTH
♠ K 9 8 4			1♦	No	1♡
♡ A 7 3		Dble	2♦	No	3♡
♦ 6		No	4♡	All pass	
♣ A Q 9 6 3					

West's lead?

For a singleton lead to be useful, partner needs to have an entry, so that the suit can be returned for you to ruff. With the strong opposition bidding plus your strong hand, it is wildly unlikely that partner has a quick entry. If you lead a diamond, the most likely outcome is that declarer will win, knock out your ace of trumps, draw trumps and discard the relevant losers on dummy's diamonds. This is precisely what would happen on the actual hand:

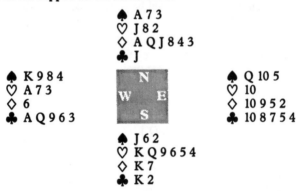

```
                    ♠ A 7 3
                    ♡ J 8 2
                    ♦ A Q J 8 4 3
                    ♣ J
  ♠ K 9 8 4              N              ♠ Q 10 5
  ♡ A 7 3          W         E          ♡ 10
  ♦ 6                                   ♦ 10 9 5 2
  ♣ A Q 9 6 3            S              ♣ 10 8 7 5 4
                    ♠ J 6 2
                    ♡ K Q 9 6 5 4
                    ♦ K 7
                    ♣ K 2
```

A trump lead would be no better and is unsound when dummy has shown a long suit (Tip 43). A low spade is the best shot. If partner has the queen, it may be an entry to return either a club (if North held ♠ A-x and ♣ J-x, for example) or a spade, whichever seems best.

A singleton or a doubleton lead against a trump contract is best reserved for very weak hands.

TIP 45:

Where dummy has not shown a long suit, if you have no clearcut lead, prefer a passive lead to leading from a suit with just one honour or two broken honours.

The clearcut attractive leads are solid three-card or longer sequences, suits headed by A-K or a singleton from a weak hand. Attacking leads which are risky are from suits like K-x-x-x, Q-x-x-x, J-x-x-x, K-J-x-x or similar. Passive leads which are reasonably safe are from two or more rags or a trump from two or three rags.

If North opens 1NT and South jumps to 4♡, what should West lead from: ♠J74 ♡86 ◇A975 ♣8643?

Where dummy bids no-trumps or simply raises partner, a long side suit in dummy is not likely. To lead a diamond from the ace would be the worst start (Tip 42) and to lead from J-x-x is almost as dangerous. A trump lead is not particularly attractive where dummy has not supported, but it is a reasonable choice on the auction. The best 'safe' lead is a club.

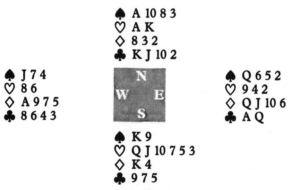

```
                    ♠ A 10 8 3
                    ♡ A K
                    ◇ 8 3 2
                    ♣ K J 10 2
    ♠ J 7 4              N              ♠ Q 6 5 2
    ♡ 8 6                              ♡ 9 4 2
    ◇ A 9 7 5      W         E         ◇ Q J 10 6
    ♣ 8 6 4 3            S             ♣ A Q
                    ♠ K 9
                    ♡ Q J 10 7 5 3
                    ◇ K 4
                    ♣ 9 7 5
```

The ace of diamonds is the usual disaster, but a spade lead could turn out worse. On the ♠4 lead—low, Q, K,—South could then finesse the ♠10, cash ♡A and ♡K, then ♠A, pitching a diamond, and ♠8, pitching the other diamond, making eleven tricks. It is true that East could withhold the ♠Q and save a trick, but that is hard to diagnose.

On a trump lead, declarer will be defeated with every finesse failing, while a club lead reaps an additional benefit:

East wins the first two tricks and switches to the ◇Q. If South covers, West wins the ace and the ◇9 would be a thoughtful continuation. When this holds the trick, West can tell not to pursue diamonds and a switch back to clubs gives East a ruff for two down.

TIP 46:

Trump length, lead length.

When you hold four or more trumps and declarer has only five or six trumps, the best strategy is usually to make declarer ruff and ruff again. If you can reduce declarer's trumps so that you have more, you may be able to draw declarer's trumps or control the play by ruffing declarer's winners and playing your winners.

How can you make declarer ruff? Your best chance is clearly your long suit, since that is where declarer figures to be shortish.

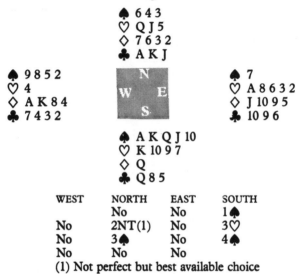

```
                    ♠ 6 4 3
                    ♡ Q J 5
                    ◇ 7 6 3 2
                    ♣ A K J
  ♠ 9 8 5 2          N          ♠ 7
  ♡ 4                            ♡ A 8 6 3 2
  ◇ A K 8 4       W   E          ◇ J 10 9 5
  ♣ 7 4 3 2          S           ♣ 10 9 6
                    ♠ A K Q J 10
                    ♡ K 10 9 7
                    ◇ Q
                    ♣ Q 8 5
```

WEST	NORTH	EAST	SOUTH
	No	No	1♠
No	2NT(1)	No	3♡
No	3♠	No	4♠
No	No	No	

(1) Not perfect but best available choice

If West leads the singleton heart or cashes a top diamond and switches to the singleton heart, West does receive a heart ruff, but that ends the defence. Declarer wins the next trick, draws trumps and claims. There can hardly be a greater indictment of the singleton lead with trump length: the singleton gets the ruff sought but to no avail.

If West leads a top diamond and continues diamonds, South ruffs and starts on trumps. After the second round, South learns of the bad break but can do nothing. If South draws West's trumps, there are two more diamond losers after conceding the ♡A. If South switches to hearts, East wins and carefully continues diamonds (if West had wanted the available heart ruff, West would have led hearts earlier). Once South ruffs, West has one trump more than South and declarer cannot escape two more losers, for if South leads hearts, West ruffs and again leads a diamond.

One of the most dramatic examples of this 'forcing defence' looks like this:

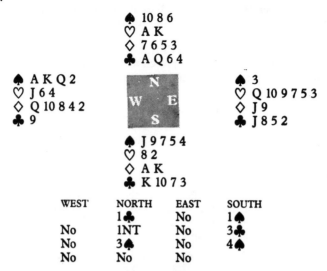

	♠ 10 8 6		
	♡ A K		
	◇ 7 6 5 3		
	♣ A Q 6 4		

```
          ♠ 10 8 6
          ♡ A K
          ◇ 7 6 5 3
          ♣ A Q 6 4
♠ A K Q 2            N            ♠ 3
♡ J 6 4                           ♡ Q 10 9 7 5 3
◇ Q 10 8 4 2     W       E        ◇ J 9
♣ 9                  S            ♣ J 8 5 2
          ♠ J 9 7 5 4
          ♡ 8 2
          ◇ A K
          ♣ K 10 7 3
```

WEST	NORTH	EAST	SOUTH
	1♣	No	1♠
No	1NT	No	3♣
No	3♠	No	4♠
No	No	No	

West would be entitled to double provided that the correct defence is found. West should not lead a singleton from a strong hand (Tip 44). See what happens on a club lead. South wins and leads a trump at every opportunity until all West's trumps are drawn. West makes just the A-K-Q of spades. Leading out the top spades achieves the same result more quickly. On the basis of trump length, lead length, West should lead a diamond. After all, if the club lead is correct it can be deferred as West has absolute control in trumps.

The diamond lead will defeat 4♠ even though South has the diamonds well held. After diamond, won by South, trump won by West (if West ducks, that is that), diamond to South, trump to West, diamond ruffed by South, South has the lead with ♠ J9 while West has ♠ A2. If South leads another trump, that is two down: West wins and continues diamonds. The best South can do is to start on clubs and allow West to ruff in for one down.

TIP 47:

When partner is marked with four or more trumps, try to adopt a forcing defence to make declarer ruff.

Just as it pays to reduce declarer's trumps when you have trump length, likewise it is a sound approach to try to force declarer to ruff when partner is marked with trump length.

WEST		WEST	NORTH	EAST	SOUTH
♠ 8 6 5			No	No	1NT(1)
♡ 7		No	2♣	No	2♡
◇ K 8 7 6 2		No	4♡	All pass	
♣ 10 7 3 2		(1) 15-17			

What should West lead?

It is likely that the opponents have reached a 4-4 heart fit and if so, partner holds four trumps. On that basis, the recommended start is your long suit, a low diamond. Even then, the defence will have to be very tight to defeat the contract.

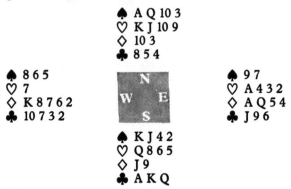

```
              ♠ A Q 10 3
              ♡ K J 10 9
              ◇ 10 3
              ♣ 8 5 4
  ♠ 8 6 5                    ♠ 9 7
  ♡ 7              N         ♡ A 4 3 2
  ◇ K 8 7 6 2    W   E       ◇ A Q 5 4
  ♣ 10 7 3 2       S         ♣ J 9 6
              ♠ K J 4 2
              ♡ Q 8 6 5
              ◇ J 9
              ♣ A K Q
```

On any lead but a diamond, declarer wins and leads trumps. East's trumps are easily drawn or, if East holds off for three rounds, South abandons trumps and plays winners in spades and clubs.

On the low diamond lead East should play the queen, although normally it is wrong to finesse against partner. Here South cannot hold a singleton ◇ K and cannot quickly dispose of the diamond loser with K-x. East can see from the points revealed that West has at most four points (see Tip 92). If the ◇ Q holds, East can tell that it would be futile to switch to clubs, as West, marked with the ◇ K, cannot hold any top club honour.

East can see three tricks via two diamonds and a heart and with no other high cards available for East-West, the only remaining hope is an extra trump trick. After ◇ Q, East cashes ◇ A and must play a third diamond, even though this concedes a ruff-and-sluff. A ruff-and-discard cannot hurt the defence if declarer's discards are winners anyway.

Declarer may ruff in either hand and start on trumps. It is vital now that East holds off with the ace of trumps for two rounds. If the ♡ A is taken earlier, another diamond will be ruffed in the short hand and declarer can cross to the other hand and draw trumps. If East has held off for two rounds, East can win the third round of trumps and now with one trump each with East and declarer, the fourth diamond forces declarer's last trump out. If declarer abandons trumps, East ruffs the third spade for one down.

If North-South reached 4♠ the demise would be swifter. With a favourable trump break evident, West would lead the singleton heart: ♡ A, heart ruff, diamond to the ace, heart ruff and now if West has the nerve to underlead the ◊ K to East's queen, the contract would be three down, while if West does the normal thing and cashes the ◊ K, that is two down.

TIP 48:

Except in extraordinary circumstances, do not lead a singleton trump.

Trump leads are normally not advisable in any event if dummy has not indicated support for declarer's suit. Where dummy may be void or singleton in declarer's suit, leading a trump may simply trap partner's trick. For instance, if the opponents have bid 1♠:1NT, 3♠:No bid a spade lead from two or three low trumps could find these layouts:

```
            x                              —
x x                J x x x  or  x x x               J x x x
       A K Q 10 x x                   A K Q 10 x x
```

and partner's probable trump trick disappears.

When dummy has shown support and no long suit, a trump lead may be attractive, but not if you hold a singleton trump. If you have a singleton, partner frequently has three or four and you may well destroy partner's likely trick if you lead the suit.

For example:

```
        K x x x                   Declarer's normal play is king
x                 Q x x            and ace, and partner's queen
        A J x x x                  would then score.

        K x x                     Without any intimation of a bad
x                 J 10 x x          break, declarer would play ace
        A Q 9 x x                   and king (or vice versa) and East
                                    scores a trick. If West leads a
```
trump, low, 10, ace, South plays back to the king, whereupon the bad break is revealed and East's remaining honour can be finessed.

```
        x x x x                   Declarer's normal play would be
x                 Q J x            to cash ace or king first, giving
        A K 10 x x                  East a trick. If West leads a
                                    trump, low, queen, ace, declarer
```
may divine the position, cross to dummy and finesse the ten, leaving partner with no trump trick.

When might you lead a singleton trump?

1. When partner passes a takeout double at the one-level, thus revealing better trumps than declarer.

2. When partner makes a penalty double of a suit at the one-level.

3. When partner makes a two-level penalty double which clearly must be based on trump length and strength.

4. Against a sacrifice bid.

TIP 49:

Lead trumps against sacrifice bids.

When your side clearly has the balance of strength, how will the opponents manage to take tricks at a level higher than justified by their high card strength? Only by making extra tricks in trumps, either via a cross-ruff or by ruffing in the short trump hand. The best defence to maximise your penalty is a trump lead at every opportunity.

Against a sacrifice, a singleton trump lead is acceptable and it may well be correct to jeopardise the chance of a trump trick by leading from trump holdings like Q-x and A-J-x.

WEST	WEST	NORTH	EAST	SOUTH
♠ 8 7	1♡	2NT*	4♡	5♣
♡ A K Q 5 2	Dble**	No	No	No
◇ 9 4 3	*Both minors, at least 5-5			
♣ A 7 6	pattern.			

**With a minimum balanced hand and strength in their suit, it is better to defend than to bid on.

West's lead?

It is tempting to lead a top heart to take a look at dummy, but in auctions such as these, that can be a costly look.

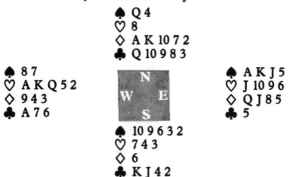

```
                    ♠ Q 4
                    ♡ 8
                    ◇ A K 10 7 2
                    ♣ Q 10 9 8 3
     ♠ 8 7                              ♠ A K J 5
     ♡ A K Q 5 2         N              ♡ J 10 9 6
     ◇ 9 4 3        W         E         ◇ Q J 8 5
     ♣ A 7 6              S             ♣ 5
                    ♠ 10 9 6 3 2
                    ♡ 7 4 3
                    ◇ 6
                    ♣ K J 4 2
```

Opposite a two-suiter, players often take a sacrifice with good support for one suit and a shortage in the other. To reduce the ruffing capacity in the support hand, trump leads are highly attractive. From A-x-x it is normal to lead a low trump (in case partner has a top honour singleton or doubleton).

On the low club lead declarer wins and plays ◇ A, ◇ K, diamond ruff. At this point West cannot be prevented from regaining the lead, and ace and another club draw South's trumps so that East will score a diamond trick to give the defence five tricks.

If West leads a top heart, declarer escapes for two off even if West switches to ace and another club. Declarer wins and continues with ◇ A, ◇ K, diamond ruff, heart ruff, diamond ruff, heart ruff, draws the last trump and cashes the fifth diamond. Down two instead of down three.

TIP 50:

Lead trumps when declarer has shown a two-suiter and you are strong in declarer's second suit.

WEST		WEST	NORTH	EAST	SOUTH
♠ A Q 10 8				No	1♠
♡ 5 4 3		No	1NT	No	2♡
◊ K 9		No	No	No	
♣ J 10 9 2					

What should West lead?

An unthinking West would light upon the sequence in clubs and start with the jack of clubs. It pays to pause and reflect on the bidding. South has shown at least five spades and four hearts and dummy's pass of 2♡ leads to a significant conclusion: dummy holds more hearts than spades, since with an equal number of cards in each major, North would have given preference to 2♠.

As dummy has fewer spades than hearts, and your spades are so strong, how will declarer eliminate the spade losers? By ruffing the spades in dummy. How can you minimise such ruffs? By leading trumps as early and as often as possible. The complete deal:

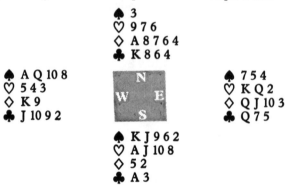

```
                  ♠ 3
                  ♡ 9 7 6
                  ◊ A 8 7 6 4
                  ♣ K 8 6 4
  ♠ A Q 10 8         N           ♠ 7 5 4
  ♡ 5 4 3      W         E       ♡ K Q 2
  ◊ K 9                          ◊ Q J 10 3
  ♣ J 10 9 2         S           ♣ Q 7 5
                  ♠ K J 9 6 2
                  ♡ A J 10 8
                  ◊ 5 2
                  ♣ A 3
```

Note what happens on the casual club lead: declarer would win in dummy to lead the singleton spade. West would win but the trump lead now would be too late. South wins, ruffs a spade, comes to the ♣A and ruffs another spade. Declarer scores two spade ruffs, three hearts in hand and the three minor suit winners.

If West leads a trump, whether South wins or ducks the first round, the defence can play three rounds of trumps before declarer can ruff a spade in dummy. Declarer will then win only three hearts and three minor tricks and will do well not to be two down.

The standard lead in trumps from West's holding is the four, followed by the three on the next round (middle-down-up in trumps). Playing high-low in trumps shows an odd number of trumps.

TIP 51:

Lead trumps when your side is known to be strong in the three suits outside trumps.

(1) WEST	WEST	NORTH	EAST	SOUTH
♠ K Q 6 4	1♦	No	1♥	2♣
♥ Q 9 3	No	No	No	
♦ A Q 9 8				
♣ 7 6				

What should West lead?

It is tempting to lead partner's suit but a one-level response has no lead-directing element since any four-card suit may be bid at the one-level. As you are so strong in spades and diamonds, it is unlikely that any heart tricks that are yours will be lost. Leading from Q-x-x is particularly risky in layouts like this:

A 10 5

Q 9 3   J 7 4 2

K 8 6

Leading the three from the queen enables declarer to make three tricks, a feat that declarer could never manage without your help.

The complete deal:

♠ 10 5 3 2
♥ A J 5 4
♦ 7 6
♣ K 8 4

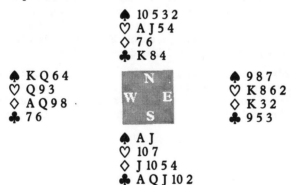

♠ K Q 6 4   ♠ 9 8 7
♥ Q 9 3   ♥ K 8 6 2
♦ A Q 9 8   ♦ K 3 2
♣ 7 6   ♣ 9 5 3

♠ A J
♥ 10 7
♦ J 10 5 4
♣ A Q J 10 2

If West leads a trump, South's tally can be contained to five clubs and the two major aces, one off. If South tries for a diamond ruff, West wins and plays a second trump. West allows East to win the next diamond to lead a third trump. East must rise with the ♦ K if declarer wins the second club in dummy and leads a diamond from table.

If West begins with a low heart, South ducks in dummy and can later finesse the jack of hearts for the contract. Likewise, on the ♠ K lead, South wins, draws trumps and can set up a second spade winner for eight tricks.

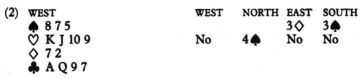

(2) WEST

♠ 8 7 5
♡ K J 10 9
♢ 7 2
♣ A Q 9 7

WEST	NORTH	EAST	SOUTH
		3♢	3♠
No	4♠	No	No

What should West lead?

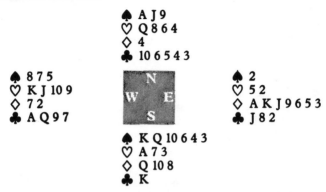

         ♠ A J 9
         ♡ Q 8 6 4
         ♢ 4
         ♣ 10 6 5 4 3

♠ 8 7 5   ♠ 2
♡ K J 10 9   ♡ 5 2
♢ 7 2   ♢ A K J 9 6 5 3
♣ A Q 9 7   ♣ J 8 2

         ♠ K Q 10 6 4 3
         ♡ A 7 3
         ♢ Q 10 8
         ♣ K

West's trumps are too weak and diamonds too long to hope for a
stunning success with a diamond lead. Again West is so strong in
hearts and clubs that any diamond tricks available are not likely to be
missed. Notice what would happen on a diamond lead. East would win
but the trump switch would be too late; South would win, ruff a
diamond, come to hand with the ace of hearts and ruff another
diamond. Coming off the table with a club, South would be able to
hold the losers to one heart, one diamond and one club.

If West leads a trump, won in dummy, East wins the diamond and
whether East switches to clubs or hearts, West will be able to lead a
second round of trumps. Declarer thus can ruff only one diamond in
dummy and careful defence will score one heart, two diamonds and a
club.

TIP 52:

Lead trumps when one opponent has shown a freak two-suiter and the other has given a preference.

WEST
♠ Q 10
♡ A K J 2
♢ A K J 10 6 5
♣ 2

Dealer West: Both vulnerable

WEST	NORTH	EAST	SOUTH
1♢	2♠*	No	3♣
3♡	5♣	No	No
No**			

*Roman jump-overcall showing spades *and* clubs, at least 5-cards in each.

**You are permitted to double if you find the right defence.

What should West lead?

Clearly North has a powerful two-suiter since South showed no enthusiasm with the 3♣ preference and may have no significant high card values at all. However, because of the 3♣ preference, South will have more clubs than spades and thus can ruff some of North's spade losers. To preserve whatever spade tricks belong to your side, you should lead a trump, even though a singleton trump lead is usually best avoided. The complete hand:

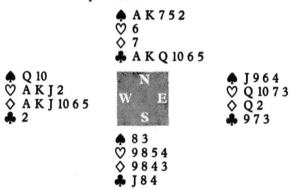

```
                    ♠ A K 7 5 2
                    ♡ 6
                    ♢ 7
                    ♣ A K Q 10 6 5
♠ Q 10                                  ♠ J 9 6 4
♡ A K J 2              N                 ♡ Q 10 7 3
♢ A K J 10 6 5    W         E            ♢ Q 2
♣ 2                       S              ♣ 9 7 3
                    ♠ 8 3
                    ♡ 9 8 5 4
                    ♢ 9 8 4 3
                    ♣ J 8 4
```

In practice, West led a top heart but that proved fatal, for the trump switch was now too late. South won the club and played ♠A, ♠K, spade ruff, heart ruff, spade ruff, heart ruff and after drawing the outstanding trumps, only a diamond and a heart were lost!

If West had led a trump, the contract could be defeated. South wins and follows with ♠A, ♠K, spade ruff, but now there is no immediate re-entry to dummy. East can win either red suit exit (West must play low to ensure East cannot go wrong) and when East continues with a trump, South's last trump is drawn, allowing the defence to score a heart, a diamond and the jack of spades for one off.

If West leads a top card from a red suit, 5♣ can be made and it would be better for East-West to sacrifice in 5♡ for one off. If your leads are good enough, however, there is no need to sacrifice at all.

TIP 53:

If the opponents have reached a 4-3 or a 4-4 trump fit and you hold five rag trumps, lead a trump.

WEST		WEST	NORTH	EAST	SOUTH
♠ A K J 10 9		1♠	Dble	No	3◇
♡ A		No	No	No	
◇ 9 5 4 3 2					
♣ Q 2					

What should West lead?

A 4-3 trump fit plays reasonably if declarer is able to ruff in the short trump hand. The strength of the 4-4 trump fit is that declarer is able to ruff in one hand and retain trump length in the other. In both cases, declarer's ruffing capacity can be minimised by repeated trump leads.

When you have five trumps and declarer is known to have five trumps, you can gain control by knocking out declarer's trumps—this is achieved by forcing declarer to ruff, usually in your long suit (see Tip 47). When declarer has fewer than five trumps and you do have five, you can eliminate declarer's trumps by repeated trump leads. The complete hand:

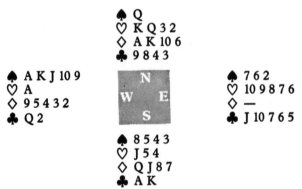

```
                    ♠ Q
                    ♡ K Q 3 2
                    ◇ A K 10 6
                    ♣ 9 8 4 3
♠ A K J 10 9                        ♠ 7 6 2
♡ A                                 ♡ 10 9 8 7 6
◇ 9 5 4 3 2                         ◇ —
♣ Q 2                               ♣ J 10 7 6 5
                    ♠ 8 5 4 3
                    ♡ J 5 4
                    ◇ Q J 8 7
                    ♣ A K
```

If West follows the tip and leads a trump from five rags, declarer will fail. If declarer wins and leads a spade, West leads a second trump. Declarer will make no more than two spade ruffs, four trumps in hand and two clubs. A similar result follows if South wins the trump and leads a heart: West wins and a second trump lead leaves declarer with eight tricks at best.

In practice, West led a top spade and smartly switched to a trump. This smartness was too late and the defence was left smarting. South won the trump shift and continued with spade ruff, club to the ace, spade ruff, club to the king, spade ruff, heart exit and made nine tricks in comfort.

TIP 54:

Lead trumps when your opponents are playing in their third-bid trump suit or fourth-bid suit.

WEST		WEST	NORTH	EAST	SOUTH
♠ 6 4				No	1◇
♡ K 10 9 7 3		No	1♡	No	1♠
◇ K Q		No	4♠	All pass	
♣ 10 9 8 5					

What should West lead?

When the opponents bid two suits and end in the third bid suit as trumps, it often indicates a cross-ruff is imminent, each opponent being shortish in the first suit bid by their partner. The best defence against an impending cross-ruff is a trump lead and usually repeated trump leads at every opportunity.

West's best lead on this reasoning is a trump. The complete hand:

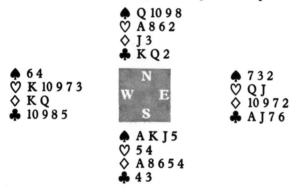

```
              ♠ Q 10 9 8
              ♡ A 8 6 2
              ◇ J 3
              ♣ K Q 2
 ♠ 6 4                        ♠ 7 3 2
 ♡ K 10 9 7 3    N            ♡ Q J
 ◇ K Q        W     E         ◇ 10 9 7 2
 ♣ 10 9 8 5      S            ♣ A J 7 6
              ♠ A K J 5
              ♡ 5 4
              ◇ A 8 6 5 4
              ♣ 4 3
```

On a trump lead, South may win and duck a diamond. A second trump follows and declarer takes the ◇ A and ruffs a diamond. Now declarer cannot leave dummy without allowing East to gain the lead and play the deadly third round of trumps, leaving declarer a trick short. The defence takes one heart, two diamonds and a club.

If West starts with the 'normal' ten of clubs and East wins the ace and returns a club, South again ducks a diamond. If West plays a third club, declarer ruffs, plays ace of diamonds, ruffs a diamond, ace of hearts and a heart exit, continuing on a cross-ruff. If West wins the diamond and switches to a trump, South wins, plays ◇ A, ruffs a diamond, club ruff, diamond ruff and a spade to hand allows South to draw trumps and cash the fifth diamond. Declarer loses one heart, one diamond and one club.

It is true that if East wins the ♣ A and switches to a trump, declarer cannot untangle the trump position later. However, why should you expect partner to do the right thing when you have not done it first?

TIP 55:

Listen to the bidding—if opponents bid and raise a suit, they usually have at least eight cards between them.

What should West lead after each of these auctions?

(A)
WEST	WEST	NORTH	EAST	SOUTH
♠ A 6			No	1♡
♡ 7 5 4	No	2◇	No	3◇
◇ A 9 3 2	No	3♡	No	4♡
♣ J 9 3 2	No	No	No	

(B)
WEST	WEST	NORTH	EAST	SOUTH
♠ Q 5			No	1♡
♡ 8 7 2	No	1NT	No	3◇
◇ 9 8 6 5 2	No	4◇	No	4♡
♣ A 7 6	No	No	No	

(C)
WEST	WEST	NORTH	EAST	SOUTH
♠ A 6			No	1♠
♡ 8 5 2	No	3♣	No	4♣
◇ J 10 9 3	No	4♠	No	4NT
♣ 7 4 3 2	No	5♠	No	6♠
	No	No	No	

(D)
WEST	WEST	NORTH	EAST	SOUTH
♠ J 10 2			No	1◇
♡ A 6	No	2NT	No	3♡
◇ J 8 7 4 3	No	4♡	No	No
♣ K 8 2	No			

(E)
WEST	WEST	NORTH	EAST	SOUTH
♠ A K 6 3			No	1♡
♡ 8 6	No	2◇	No	3◇
◇ 10 7 4 3 2	No	4♡	No	No
♣ 8 6	No			

Solutions:

(A) North-South appear to hold eight diamonds, leaving partner with a singleton. Lead the ◇ A and continue with the *nine* of diamonds for partner to ruff. The *nine* asks for a spade return (high card, high suit when giving a ruff). You expect to take ◇ A, diamond ruff, ♠ A, diamond ruff plus any tricks partner can contribute.

(B) North-South have shown eight diamonds and South probably has six hearts–four diamonds, such as A7, KQJ954, AK73, 5. Partner is thus void in diamonds and you lead the *two* to ask for a club return (low card, low suit). The normal rules on leads (fourth-highest, etc.) do not apply when you expect partner to ruff the lead. You plan to take a diamond ruff, ♣ A, diamond ruff and hope partner can produce at least one more trick.

(C) The opposition bidding suggests eight clubs, giving partner at most a singleton. Lead a club and on gaining the lead with the ♠ A give partner a club ruff. The 'natural' jack of diamonds lead would be normal except for the revealing information from the bidding. Even though you expect to defeat 6♠, do not double. They may run to 6NT which you may be unable to beat.

(D) South's bidding suggests five diamonds–four hearts. North's 2NT reveals at least two diamonds leaving partner at most a singleton. Further analysis suggests partner is void: North holds four hearts presumably, so why was the 2NT response chosen? Probably because the hand pattern is 3-4-3-3. If that is so and South has five diamonds, partner will be void. Lead the *three* of diamonds (low card, low suit), asking for a club return.

(E) Again partner seems to be void in diamonds. What a lucky fellow to have you as partner. Lead the *ten* of diamonds, asking for a spade back (high card, high suit). You expect to take a diamond ruff, ♠ K, diamond ruff, ♠ A, diamond ruff, plus anything partner can contribute.

It would be an error to lead ♠ K, intending to follow with a diamond. Firstly, if dummy or declarer has a singleton spade, you would be unable to regain the lead for a second diamond ruff: secondly, if you can cash two spades, the spade lead eliminates an entry and means you can give partner only two diamond ruffs instead of three.

TIPS 56-80:   Declarer Play

TIP 56:

Apply the Even Suit Break Test when deciding to play for the drop or the finesse.

Some hands require no more than a key suit be handled to best advantage. You need to know the correct technique for handling basic card combinations. Once you know the correct technique, you can progress to judging when it is best to depart from the 'book' play.

The Even Suit Break Test:

Step 1: Assume the missing cards divide as evenly as possible.

Step 2: Place the missing key card with the longer holding in the opponent's hand. e.g. If the even-break is 3-2, place the missing key card with the 3-card holding: if the even-break is 2-1, assume the missing card is doubleton, not singleton.

Step 3: Check whether the missing honour will drop if it is with the longer holding. If the honour will not drop, take the finesse.

The correct play on this basis will not work all the time but does succeed most of the time.

Should you finesse or play for the drop with these combinations:

Dummy	(1) 8 6 5 4	(2) 8 6 5 4 3	(3) 8 6 5 4 3
Declarer	A Q 9 7 2	A Q 9 7 2	A Q J 9 7 2

Solutions: (1) 4 cards missing—even-break 2-2—king figures to be doubleton—king unlikely to fall under ace—take the finesse.

(2) 3 cards missing—even-break 2-1—king figures to be doubleton—probably will not drop under ace—finesse.

(3) 2 cards missing—even-break 1-1—king likely to be singleton—probably will drop under ace—play the ace rather than finesse.

What is the best play with these combinations?

Dummy	(4) A 6 4 2	(5) A 6 4 2	(6) 9 8 6 4 2
Declarer	K J 7 3	K J 7 5 3	A K J 5 3

Solutions: (4) 5 cards missing—even-break 3-2—queen likely to be tripleton more often than doubleton—queen is therefore unlikely to fall if you play ace and king—best is to finesse (ace first, then finesse jack). When finessing for a queen it is usual to *finesse on the second round of the suit* (top honour first, finesse on the next round).

(5) 4 cards missing—even-break 2-2—queen likely to be doubleton—therefore is likely to drop if you play ace and king—reject the finesse.

(6) 3 cards missing—even break 2-1—queen likely to be doubleton and if so, will fall under ace and king—do not finesse on the first round (could lose to a singleton queen). Play the ace: if all follow, the queen will fall under the king; if left-hand opponent shows out, cross to dummy in another suit and then finesse the jack; if right-hand opponent shows out, you have an inevitable loser . . . somebody up there doesn't like you.

How do you manage these holdings to give yourself the best chance of no loser?

Dummy	(7) 8 4	(8) 8 4	(9) 8 4
Declarer	A K Q 10 6 2	A K Q 10 6	A K Q 10

Solutions: (7) 5 missing—even break 3-2—jack likely to be tripleton—play ace, king, queen—do not finesse the 10.

(8) 6 cards missing—even break 3-3—jack likely to be tripleton—play ace, king, queen—do not finesse the 10.

(9) 7 cards missing—even break 4-3—J-x-x-x more likely than J-x-x. The jack is therefore not likely to drop if you play ace, king, queen. Play the ace, cross to dummy in another suit and then finesse the 10 as the best chance for no loser.

Caution: The correct technique in one particular suit may not be the correct approach to the whole hand.

TIP 57:

When cashing winners in a suit, keep the tenace intact.

'Tenace': Non-touching honours in the same suit such as A-Q, A-J,
A-10, K-J, K-10, Q-10. More broadly, any holding of cards
not in sequence in the same suit.

When you have a tenace, you have an opportunity to finesse. If you
have winners in dummy and winners in hand, you play off first the
winners where there is no tenace. Retain the tenace as long as you can.
By following this approach, you may be able to cope with a bad break.

What is the correct play with these holdings:

Dummy	(1) A J 6 4 2	(2) A 9 6 4 2	(3) A J 9 2
Declarer	K 8 7 5 3	K J 7 5 3	K 7 5 4 3

Solutions: (1) Play the king first—retain the A-J tenace. If West has
Q-10-9 you are able to finesse the jack. (If East has Q-10-9 a loser is
inevitable).

(2) Play the ace first—retain the K-J tenace. If East has Q-10-9, you
can finesse the jack next.

(3) Play the king first—retain the A-J tenace. If all follow it is normal
to play the ace next (see Tip 56), but if East shows out, you can finesse
the 9 next and finesse the jack later.

How about these combinations?

Dummy	(4) A 10 7 2	(5) A Q 5 2	(6) Q 10 5 4
Declarer	K Q 5 3	K 10 7 3	A K 3 2

Solutions: (4) Play the king, then the queen—retain the A-10 tenace. If
West began with J-x-x-x, East will show out on the second round and
you are able to finesse the 10 and avoid a loser. If West has J-x-x-x,
and you play the ace first, you have a loser.

(5) Play the ace, then the queen—retain the K-10 tenace. If East began
with J-x-x-x, you are able to finesse the 10.

(6) Play the ace, then king—retain the Q-10 tenace.

TIP 58:

Retain the near-tenace.

Just as best technique is to retain the tenace as long as possible (Tip 57), if there is no obvious tenace there is still a correct order in which winners should be cashed. Check the winners in your hand and dummy and note which hand contains the card closest to a winner. Treat that combination as a 'near-tenace' and play the winners *from the other hand* first. Keep the near-tenace intact as long as possible.

For example:

Dummy	K Q 3 2	In which order should you play
Declarer	A 9 5 4	your winners?

The nearest card to a winner is the 9—treat the A-9 as a near-tenace and therefore play off first the king and the queen. If the suit breaks 3-2, your virtuosity proves unnecessary but your reward comes when the layout is like this:

	K Q 3 2		If you play the ace on the first or
J		10 8 7 6	second round (breaking your
	A 9 5 4		tenace), East wins a trick with the
			10. By playing the king then the

queen, West shows out on the second round and you have the A-9 over East's 10-8 and can finesse the 9 for no loser.

Dummy:	A 7 3 2	How do you handle this suit to
Declarer:	K 9 6 4	hold your losers to one trick only, if possible?

Solution: The 9 is closer to a winner than the 7. Therefore retain the K-9 initially and play the ace first. If West drops an honour card, lead low and insert the 9 if East plays low. If the suit breaks 3-2, such as:

	A 7 3 2		The 9 loses to West but the king
Q J		10 8 5	captures East's remaining card.
	K 9 6 4		Your reward comes on a division like this:

	A 7 3 2		If you play the king first
J		Q 10 8 5	(breaking your near tenace), East
	K 9 6 4		scores *two* tricks. If you play the ace first and play towards your

K-9, if East plays the 8, your 9 wins and you lose one trick only. If East plays an honour, you win the king and, as West shows out, you cross to dummy in another suit to lead towards your 9-6 over East's Q-8, again restricting East to one trick.

TIP 59:

You are missing J-10-x-x or J-x-x-x. If you hold equivalent tenaces or near-tenaces, retain as many winners in one hand as there are missing honours.

These situations are treated identically:

Dummy	(1) K 10 4 3	(2) K Q 10 3	(3) Q 9 4 3
Declarer	A Q 9 5 2	A 9 5 4 2	A K 10 6 2

In each case you have three winners, and as the 10 and 9 are touching cards K-10 tenace is equivalent to the A-9 or Q-9 tenace. As there is only *one* honour missing, keep *one* winner in each hand. Accordingly, in (1) play the ace or queen first (not the king); in (2) play the king or queen first (not the ace); and in (3) play the ace or king first (not the queen). If the suit does break 4-0, you are able to finesse against either opponent.

These situations are also treated identically:

Dummy	(4) K Q 9 2	(5) A Q 8 3 2	(6) Q 8 3 2
Declarer	A 8 5 4 3	K 9 5 4	A K 9 5 4

In each case you have three winners, the 9 and the 8 produce equivalent near-tenaces. However, as *two* honours are missing, you must retain *two* honours to capture the jack and ten if there is a 4-0 break. Thus in (1), play the ace first—if West does hold J-10-7-6, you can lead twice towards K-Q-9 if necessary to avoid a loser. In (2), play the king first, retaining the A-Q-8 in case West started with J-10-7-6. In (3), play the queen first, guarding against J-10-7-6 with East. If a 4-0 break exists but the J-10-x-x lie over your two honours, such as—

	Q 8 3 2	
J 10 7 6		—
	A K 9 5 4	

you are unable to escape a loser. If you lead low from hand, West plays the ten or jack to ensure a trick.

TIP 60:

Declarer should normally win or attempt to win a trick with the highest of equal cards.

Example:

```
                    Dummy
                    6 4 2
West leads the 5                        East plays the jack
                    A K Q
                    Declarer
```

Declarer should win the ace. It is immaterial to declarer as the A, K and Q are all winners, but by winning with the ace you make it harder for the defenders to know what is going on.

Suppose the layout is in fact:

```
                    6 4 2
    10 8 7 5 3                          J 9
                    A K Q
```

If you win with the Q, West knows that you hold the ace and king and that the jack is East's highest. West may later switch to a suit more dangerous to you. If you win with the ace, West must consider that the position is as above or perhaps one of these two:

```
        6 4 2                               6 4 2
10 8 7 5 3        Q J    or    10 8 7 5 3            K Q J
        A K 9                               A 9
```

In each case, East's correct play is the jack (third-hand-high, but cheapest of equally high cards). If defenders have to guess at the position, they will sometimes guess wrongly.

Similarly:

```
                    8 3
West leads the 4              East plays the 10
                    A Q J
```

Win with the queen, not with the jack.

```
                    7 5
West leads the 3             East plays the 9
                    A K J 10
```

Win with the jack, not with the 10.

The same principle applies when you are taking a finesse with equal cards in hand:

Dummy   7 4 3

Declarer   A Q J 10 5

You lead the 3 from dummy, East plays the 2 and you play . . . ?

The correct card is the queen. If the finesse works, it is irrelevant to you whether you finesse the queen, jack or ten; if it loses, the actual card chosen is irrelevant to you. It is not irrelevant to the defenders. By finessing the queen you obscure the location of the jack and ten.

Suppose the position is:

```
              7 4 3
9 6                        K 8 2
              A Q J 10 5
```

If you finesse the 10 and it holds the trick, East knows West cannot have the queen or jack. If you finesse the queen and it holds, East cannot be sure who has the jack or ten.

Again, if the position is:

```
              7 4 3
K 9                        8 6 2
              A Q J 10 5
```

If you finesse the 10 and West wins the king, East would know that West does not hold the queen or jack (a defender wins with the cheapest card possible, so if West wins the 10 with the king, that denies the queen and jack). If you finesse the queen and West takes the king, East cannot tell who has the jack or ten.

The more you keep them guessing, the more mistakes they will make.

TIP 61:

When more than one suit offers the chance to make your contract and it is dangerous to allow the opponents in, first try those possibilities which do not risk losing the lead.

(1)
WEST	EAST	WEST	EAST
♠ 7 6 3	♠ K 4	1NT(1)	2♣(2)
♡ A K 3	♡ Q 5 4 2	2◊	3NT
◊ A 4	◊ K Q 10 2	(1) 16-18	
♣ A Q 9 4 3	♣ J 10 5	(2) Stayman	

North leads ♠5. You hold your breath as you play the king. It holds. How do you continue?

(2)
WEST	EAST	WEST	EAST
♠ A K J 9	♠ 10 3	2NT	3♣
♡ A 9 4	♡ J 5	3♠	4NT
◊ A 6 2	◊ K Q 9 4 3	5♣	6NT
♣ A J 3	♣ K Q 10 4		

North leads ♡K. Plan West's play.

Solutions: (1) After the ♠K, West has 8 top winners. The 'instinctive' play of the club finesse is too risky yet. If it loses, you have no further chance to test either red suit for the ninth trick. Test the hearts first, ♡A, ♡K, heart to the queen. If hearts are 3-3, your ninth trick has materialised with the thirteenth heart. If the hearts are not 3-3, try the diamonds next: ace first, then low to the king followed by the queen. This is not a case where you follow the normal technique of finessing the 10 (see Tip 56). If the jack of diamonds has dropped, the ◊10 is your ninth trick. If the hearts are not 3-3, and the ◊10 is not high, lead the ♣J and let it run if South plays low. You take the club finesse *as the last resort*.

(2) You have ten top tricks. The two extra can come from two spade finesses or a favourable diamond break. As you have no entry problems, you may as well run your club winners and discard a heart. Defenders do sometimes discard badly. Follow with a diamond to the ace and a diamond to the king (keeping your Q-9 near-tenace). If diamonds are 3-2 or if South started with the bare 10 or the bare jack in diamonds, you have five diamond tricks.

If diamonds do not behave, lead the ♠10 and let it run, repeating the finesse if it works. When you wish to finesse for the queen but you have only two cards opposite AKJ10, AKJ10x, or AKJ10xx (or equivalent holdings), it is better to take two finesses than to cash a top honour first and take only one finesse later.

TIP 62:

As soon as dummy appears, count dummy's points and your own. Deduct the total from 40 and you can often tell where the missing points are.

(1)

WEST	EAST	WEST	NORTH	EAST	SOUTH
♠ K J 9 8 5	♠ A Q 4			1♡	1NT	No
♡ J 2	♡ A K	3♠	No	4♠	No
◇ 6 5 4	◇ Q J 10	No	No	No	
♣ A Q 4	♣ 8 7 6 3 2				

North leads ◇ K, ◇ A and a third diamond, all following. Plan West's play. Trumps turn out to be 3-2.

(2)

WEST	EAST	WEST	NORTH	EAST	SOUTH
♠ K 10 8 4	♠ Q J 7 2			1♡	Dble	No
♡ A 3	♡ J 2	2♠	No	4♠	No
◇ J 7 5 2	◇ A K Q	No	No		
♣ Q 7 4	♣ K 6 5 3				

North leads the ♡ K, won by your ace. A spade is won by North who cashes the ♡ Q and exits with a spade, South following. North discards a heart on the next spade. Plan the play.

Solutions: (1) You have 11 points, dummy has 16, 40-27=13 HCP missing, almost all with North for the opening. The ♣ K therefore will be with North. You cannot afford to lose two club tricks. Do not take a finesse that is known to lose (see Tip 63). Draw trumps and continue with ♣ A and a low club, praying for North to hold ♣ K-x. If North began with something like ♠ 73, ♡ Q 109543, ◇ AK8, ♣ K9 you make your game, which would fail if you finessed the ♣ Q.

(2) You have 10 HCP, dummy has 16 HCP, 14 HCP are missing. You have lost two tricks and must lose a club trick. You must avoid losing two club tricks. As North opened, North will hold the ace of clubs. The only legitimate chance is that North has the ♣ A singleton or doubleton.

Win the third spade in hand and lead a low club towards dummy's king. If North's ace appears, your problems are over. If North plays low and the king wins, play a club from dummy *and play low from hand.* Do not play the queen. If you play the queen and it loses to the ace, their jack or ten will be high. If North began with something like ♠ A3, ♡ KQ 10964, ◇ 863, ♣ A9 your queen will be high after the ♣ A drops doubleton.

If North began with A-8-2 or A-10-8-2 or better in clubs, you never had a chance for success. You just have to pray that North has the ♣ A short.

TIP 63:

Abandon the normal technique in handling a suit if you can tell that it will not work.

(1)

WEST	EAST	WEST	NORTH	EAST	SOUTH
♠ Q J 10 6 4	♠ A 7 5 3		No	No	No
♡ 8 6	♡ 10 4 3 2	1♠	2♡	3♠	No
◊ K Q 2	◊ A 7	4♠	No	No	No
♣ A Q 5	♣ K 8 3				

North leads the ♡ K and ♡ Q, South playing 9, then 5. North switches to the 10 of clubs. How should West continue?

(2)

WEST	EAST	WEST	NORTH	EAST	SOUTH
♠ A J 10 7 3	♠ K 5 4 2				1♡
♡ 8 6	♡ 10 7	1♠	No	3♠	No
◊ Q J 2	◊ A K 5 4	4♠	No	No	No
♣ K J 7	♣ Q 8 6				

North leads the ace of hearts and a low heart is won by South's jack. South cashes the ace of clubs and West wins the club continuation. How should West continue?

Solutions: (1) West should start on spades. The normal play missing the king is to lead the queen and take the finesse. That play is bound to lose here. North's 2♡ bid will be based on five hearts, and after the first two tricks, North's hearts initially must have been A-K-Q-J-7, North passed as dealer and could not hold the ♠ K as well—that would be 13 points.

Do not take a finesse that is certain to lose. Play a spade to the ace and another spade. If South began with ♠ K singleton, you have an overtrick. If South has K-x or K-x-x, you still make your contract. There is a risk in finessing in spades: if North started with a singleton club and you took the losing finesse, South could give North a club ruff for one off.

(2) You have lost 3 tricks and cannot afford to lose a trump trick. Normal technique here is to play king and ace and hope the queen drops. However, South is marked with the ♠ Q: you hold 12 HCP and so does dummy. North led the ♡ A, leaving 12 HCP missing. Since South opened in first seat, it is logical to credit South with the remaining 12 HCP. Without the ♠ Q, South would have only 10 HCP for the opening.

Play a spade to the king and a spade back. If South follows low, finesse the jack.

A bridge player never follows rules blindly.

TIP 64:

Do not play an honour if it cannot win the trick or cannot promote a winner for yourself or partner.

The purpose of playing high cards is to win tricks or to build up tricks. If a card cannot fulfil either of these functions it is a waste to play it.

WEST	EAST	WEST	NORTH	EAST	SOUTH
♠ 8	♠ K 4 3 2			No	No
♡ A Q 8 6 5 4	♡ K J 9 2	1♡	No	3♡	No
◇ A 7 5	◇ K J 2	6♡	No	No	No
♣ A K 7	♣ 8 4				

North leads the ♠Q. Plan West's play.

North's ♠Q lead marks the ace with South. Nobody leads the ♠Q from AQJx against the slam! There is no point therefore in playing the ♠K on the queen—it cannot win and it cannot build up a spade winner for you. To play the king is futile, yet how often do we hear players say, 'I wanted to force out the ace'. Why? Forcing an ace out does you no good if it does not help you win a trick.

The South hand may well be like this: ♠A96 ♡7 ◇Q1083 ♣Q10652.

If the ♠K is played at trick one, West will ultimately take the diamond finesse. One down.

If West ducks the spade lead, ruffs a second low spade (now or later), draws trumps ending in dummy and leads a third low spade, ruffing, South's ace happens to drop and leaves the ♠K high to allow a diamond discard, making the diamond finesse unnecessary.

WEST	EAST	WEST	NORTH	EAST	SOUTH
♠ 7 2	♠ A 8 6 4		3♠	No	No
♡ A K Q 8 7 6 3	♡ J 10	4♡	No	No	No
◇ Q	◇ 8 5 4 2				
♣ A 9 7	♣ K 8 4				

North leads the ♠K. Plan West's play.

Did you play the ace of spades? If so, you have missed the point of the tip: do not play an honour if it cannot win. The ♠A will be ruffed by South, *of course*, if North holds the seven spades expected for the 3♠ opening. You will then win only seven hearts and two clubs. Play low on the first spade and on the next spade if North continues. If a third spade is led, play low in dummy and ruff in hand, draw trumps and you will still be able to use the ♠A later for your tenth trick. South's hand:

♠ — ♡ 9 5 4 ◇ A K 9 7 ♣ J 10 6 5 3 2

TIP 65:

To obtain a genuine count in a suit headed by the A-K-Q, lead the king, not the ace.

WEST	EAST	WEST	EAST
♠ A K Q 10	♠ 6 5 4	1NT	3NT
♡ K 8 6	♡ A 5 3	No	
♢ 9 8 7	♢ A K 6		
♣ 6 5 3	♣ A 7 4 2		

North leads the ♡ Q. Plan West's play.

Declarer has eight winners and needs four spade tricks for the contract. If the jack of spades does not fall in the first two rounds declarer will have to judge whether to finesse or play for the drop on the third round. The percentage play is to play for the jack to drop (see Tip 56) but you prefer to make the winning decision at the table and not rely purely on probabilities.

Competent defenders are used to signalling the count when declarer is tackling a suit (standard count is high-low with an even number, lowest with an odd number).

If the opponents are avid and trustworthy count signallers, you can enlist their aid. If you play off ♠ A and ♠ K, you are advertising your strength and North may not signal length. If you start with the king first, North may expect South to hold the ace and may commence a high-low signal with a doubleton. If North does play high-low when you continue with the queen and you feel North is not a very deceptive defender, you have enough evidence to cross to dummy and finesse the ten of spades.

Do not weep on partner's shoulder, however, if North fooled you by playing high-low with J-x-x. Just jot North's name in your little black book under 'Opponents To Be Treated With Respect' and do not rely on this North's count signals next time.

The same advice applies if the holding is:

Dummy	Q 7 2	Lead the king from hand first
Declarer	A K 10 6	rather than the ace and rather than low to the queen first.

The king is more likely to give you true count from both opponents. If you obtain conflicting count signals, prefer to rely on the signal from the second player. Fourth player can often judge from partner's play what is happening and may give a fake count signal to try to put you off the track.

TIP 66:

Pay very close attention to the bidding. You can calculate the distribution of the cards very accurately if the opponents use off-beat methods to show unusual shapes.

Dealer North: East-West vulnerable.

WEST	EAST		WEST	NORTH	EAST	SOUTH
♠ A	♠ K J 8 7			2♠*	Dble	3♣
♡ J 10 8 5 4	♡ A K Q 3		3♡	5♣	6♡	No
◇ J 9 6 5	◇ A 7 2		No	No		
♣ K 9 3	♣ A 4					

*Unusual two-suiter, both majors *or* both minors, at least 5-5, 6-11 HCP

North leads ♣Q. Plan the play.

Suppose you win the ♣A and play ♡A, ♡K, ♡Q. South follows and North discards two clubs on the second and third heart. How should West continue?

Suppose that West elects to continue with the king of clubs and a club ruff. South follows to the king but discards a low spade on the third club. What now?

Once you refer to the original bidding the whole hand is a read-out. North began with six clubs (already known as South showed out on the third round) and five diamonds (from the meaning of the unusual 2♠ opening). That is eleven cards and North followed to one heart, so the rest is easy as South must hold at least seven spades. Play a spade to the ace and all is known.

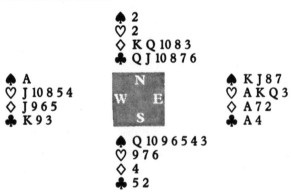

```
              ♠ 2
              ♡ 2
              ◇ K Q 10 8 3
              ♣ Q J 10 8 7 6
♠ A                          ♠ K J 8 7
♡ J 10 8 5 4      N          ♡ A K Q 3
◇ J 9 6 5      W     E       ◇ A 7 2
♣ K 9 3           S          ♣ A 4
              ♠ Q 10 9 6 5 4 3
              ♡ 9 7 6
              ◇ 4
              ♣ 5 2
```

Once you know North's pattern, you can easily calculate South's and the remaining cards after drawing trumps and ruffing out the clubs will be:

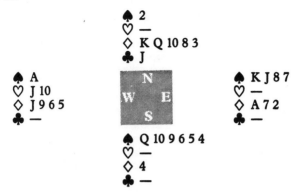

```
                    ♠ 2
                    ♡ —
                    ◇ K Q 10 8 3
                    ♣ J

    ♠ A              N            ♠ K J 8 7
    ♡ J 10       W       E        ♡ —
    ◇ J 9 6 5                     ◇ A 7 2
    ♣ —              S            ♣ —

                    ♠ Q 10 9 6 5 4
                    ♡ —
                    ◇ 4
                    ♣ —
```

A spade to the ace is followed by a diamond to the ace, and as South is known to have only spades left, you lead the 8 of spades, allowing South to win as you discard a diamond. South must play a spade into dummy's K-J tenace allowing you to discard your remaining diamonds.

Easy once you count North's cards.

TIP 67:

When you are trying to sneak a trick as declarer, lead the second card from a sequence in hand against a strong defender, bottom card from a sequence in hand against a weak defender.

There are many occasions where you wish to sneak a trick past a defender. In 3NT with a suit wide open, you want to snatch the ninth trick before the defenders realise where the weakness lies. Fearing a ruff in a trump contract you want to lead two rounds of trumps and may wish to sneak one round of trumps from K-Q-J-10-5 opposite 7-4-3-2 without losing to the ace. Leading the king will not work. Against a strong defender, the lead of the queen may cause second player to duck with the ace, in case partner holds the singleton king. Against a weak defender the 10 will usually work, since the weak defender is conditioned to play second hand low and will hope partner can beat the 10.

Example 1: Dealer North: North-South vulnerable.

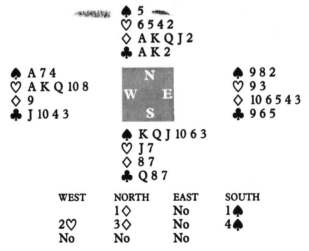

	WEST	NORTH	EAST	SOUTH
		1♦	No	1♠
	2♡	3♦	No	4♠
	No	No	No	

The defence can beat 4♠. After two top hearts, West leads a third heart, ruffed by East's 8 and overruffed by the 10. West wins the top trump exit and plays another heart, East ruffs with the 9, overruffed by South again. South now has only one top trump and after cashing it, West's ♠7 is the master trump. One down. The defence has executed a neat double uppercut.

Declarer cannot avoid this legitimately but can try to dissuade West from winning the first round of trumps. After overruffing East's 8, South should *not* lead the king of spades. Lead the queen against a good defender, the jack against a poor defender. If West falls for it and plays low, the next top trump draws East's last trump, the second uppercut evaporates and West's ♠7 can be drawn safely.

Example 2: Dealer South: Both vulnerable.

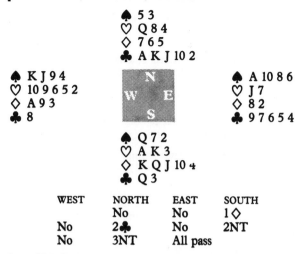

```
                ♠ 5 3
                ♡ Q 8 4
                ◇ 7 6 5
                ♣ A K J 10 2
♠ K J 9 4            N            ♠ A 10 8 6
♡ 10 9 6 5 2                      ♡ J 7
◇ A 9 3        W        E         ◇ 8 2
♣ 8                 S            ♣ 9 7 6 5 4
                ♠ Q 7 2
                ♡ A K 3
                ◇ K Q J 10 4
                ♣ Q 3
```

WEST	NORTH	EAST	SOUTH
	No	No	1◇
No	2♣	No	2NT
No	3NT	All pass	

West leads ♡5. Declarer has 8 winners and if South cashes the hearts and the clubs, the defence cannot miss the need for spade tricks. Declarer's best chance is to try to sneak a diamond trick before the defence realises the urgency to tackle spades. South should play low in dummy and win the jack with the ace so that West may hope East started with K-J-x over the queen.

Once you win in hand, it also does not pay you to cross to dummy for a diamond lead, as that would indicate your clubs are solid. Best to lead a diamond from hand, the 10 against weak opposition, the queen against a good defender. Most weak defenders in the West seat will duck if you lead the *ten* of diamonds and you have your ninth trick. (Do not get greedy and try another diamond!) Even if West takes the ace, most weak defenders will continue the hearts and now you have a bonanza.

◇ 10 will not fool a strong West. When declarer leads an honour and you have the card below it, this is a sure sign declarer is trying to sneak a trick. Staring at the 9 of diamonds, a good defender will know what you are up to, will grab the ◇ A and switch swiftly and successfully to the 4 of spades. Make your diamond play believable by leading the queen and you may survive or you may not— a good defender did not become good by letting declarers steal contracts.

TIP 68:

Make the most of the inferences given to you by the opening lead.

There is a wealth of information available from the opening lead and a discerning declarer can draw valuable inferences in this area.

1. How fast was the lead? A defender with a naturally attractive lead will play at normal pace. When there is a significant hesitation before the lead, declarer may deduce that the defender has no clearcut lead and has some holdings which are undesirable to lead from.

2. A trump lead normally indicates trumps are splitting evenly (a trump lead is uncommon from a 4-card holding—trump length, lead length: Tip 46).

3. A player who leads a long suit bid by dummy or a second suit bid by declarer is almost always leading a singleton.

WEST	EAST	WEST	EAST
♠ 8 7	♠ A Q 9 3 2		1♠
♡ A 8 7 6 4	♡ K 3 2	2♡	3♡
◇ A K Q 6	◇ 7 5	4◇	4♡
♣ K 4	♣ Q J 7	No	

North leads ♠4. Plan the play.

Do not be fooled into finessing the ♠Q. The consequence will be South wins the king, gives North a spade ruff, and a club to South's ace is followed by another spade, promoting a trump trick for the defence. Win ♠A and play ♡K, ♡A. As long as trumps break, you are home.

4. When the opening leader has bid a suit but does not lead it and you have J-x-x in dummy and x-x-x in hand (or similarly weak holdings), the opening leader's suit is headed by the A-Q.

5. When dummy has shown a longish side suit and the lead is a trump, the defender on lead is strong in dummy's long suit. A trump lead would not be made if there was a fear that dummy's long suit would run and provide discards.

6. When declarer bids two suits and dummy gives a preference, a trump lead usually indicates the leader is strong in declarer's other suit.

7. Against no-trumps, if the opening lead is from a four-card suit, the leader will not hold a longer suit. After 1NT:3NT, North leads ♠2.

WEST	EAST	
♠ 10 7 4	♠ A 9 5	You win with the ace and when
♡ A K Q 10	♡ J 3 2	you play hearts, North discards a
◇ A 8 4	◇ K Q 10 7	club on the second round. How
♣ 6 5 3	♣ Q J 8	do you tackle the diamonds?

North's ♠2 is from a 4-card suit, so North has four spades and one heart, the eight minor cards must be 4◇–4♣, or else North would have preferred to lead from a 5-card suit. When you play ◇K, diamond to the ace and a third diamond, play the ◇10 if North plays low. The diamond position is not a guess.

8. If a low card is led in a trump contract, assume the leader does not hold the ace.

Dummy	K 6	If a low card is led against your trump contract, play dummy's 6, not the king. The ace is on the right almost all the time.
Declarer	J 4	

9. If you can tell the lead is risky, such as leading an unsupported ace or from holdings like K-x-x, Q-x-x, J-x-x-x, the leader has dangerous holdings in all suits.

10. If the lead is very unusual, see what follows.

Dummy	♡ J 6	You are in 4♠ after left hand opponent opened 3♡. The lead is the *two* of hearts. What do you make of that?
Declarer	♡ 7 4	

The *two* of hearts cannot be a normal lead (it cannot be fourth highest as West should hold seven hearts). A wildly abnormal lead is used as a suit-preference signal—in the case of a pre-empt, it usually signifies a void. In this case you should read the ♡2 as a signal that West is void in clubs. Also you should play the jack from dummy. Desperate defenders when holding a side void have been known to lead away from suits like AKQ8532 hoping to hit partner's jack as an entry.

TIP 69:

When playing K-Q-10 in hand opposite rags in dummy, play low to the queen first, *not the king*—to tempt the defender with the ace sitting over you to take the ace and spare you the guess on the next round.

(1)
```
            8 4 3
A 9 5                 J 7 6 2
            K Q 10
```
(2)
```
            8 4 3
J 7 6 2                 A 9 5
            K Q 10
```

If you know the location of the ace and jack, the K-Q-10 holding can always be played for two tricks (unless there is A-J-x offside). The problem is that you usually play low to the king, which holds, cross back to dummy and lead low and when second player plays low, you have to decide whether to finesse the 10 (wins in layout 1, loses in 2) or whether to rise with the queen (loses in 1, wins in 2).

Because declarer is unlikely to lead to an unsupported king if anything else is offering, a defender generally knows that if a low card from dummy is led to declarer's king, declarer has more than just the king. Consequently, good defenders can usually duck smoothly in situation 1, leaving you with the nasty guess on the second round of the suit.

You can frequently catch a defender out by leading low to your *queen*. Firstly, they now may expect that partner holds the king and will not wish to duck. If they win the ace, you can finesse the 10 later. Secondly, caught unawares by the queen rather than the expected king, they may not be able to duck smoothly. You may be able to diagnose a defender's dilemma even if they do eventually duck. Again you would cross to dummy and finesse the 10 next.

TIP 70:

Whenever possible, play your suit combinations to prevent the defenders signalling. If a trick is sure to be lost when you are setting up a long suit or drawing trumps, lose it early to minimise the opportunity for the defenders to signal.

WEST	EAST	WEST	NORTH	EAST	SOUTH
♠ A K	♠ Q 9 4	1♢	No	2♢	No
♡ Q 6	♡ 5 4 2	3NT	No	No	No
♢ A 8 6 4 3	♢ 10 9 7 5 2				
♣ K Q 6 2	♣ A 7				

North leads ♣ J. Plan West's play.

With only 7 tricks, West must develop the diamonds but that involves losing the lead and if the defence finds the heart switch, it is curtains for you. Faced with this unpalatable situation, some macho declarers win the ♣A and lead a heart, attacking the weak holding and hoping the defence will therefore abandon any attack in that area.

You should resort to such measures only in utter desperation. That is not the case here where you have reasonable chances on normal lines. Declarer's best shot is:

(1) Win the ♣A and play the six from hand. If you win in hand, your club strength is revealed; if you play the 2, not the 6, South's 5 is clearly the lowest, a discouraging signal. By concealing the 2, you may persuade North that South's 5 might be encouraging, say from Q52.

(2) Play a diamond *and duck it*, hoping North wins the trick. Suppose North started with ♠J63 ♡A97 ♢KQ ♣J10943. North wins the first diamond and will have to be very bright to find the killing switch to hearts. It is important to give the lead to North: if a defender did not hit the killing lead early, it is not likely that the killing switch will be found later without a signal from partner. If you win ♢A and exit a diamond, South is able to signal the strength in hearts and now the switch from North is highly likely. By ducking the first diamond, you prevent South's signal.

Ducking the diamond is also vital if North has the bare king of diamonds. Otherwise ♢A and another diamond allow South on lead and South is much more likely to switch to hearts. When giving up the lead, prefer to give it to a weak defender, not a strong defender—prefer to give it to the defender who is unlikely to know the position, not to the one who probably knows what to do.

TIP 71:

After an opposing pre-empt, play for any critical cards in the other suits to be with the partner of the pre-emptor.

(1)

WEST	EAST	WEST	NORTH	EAST	SOUTH
♠ A 8 7 4 3	♠ K 5 2			No	3♢
♡ A J 5 4	♡ K 10 9 3 2	Dble*	No	4♡	No
♢ 7 2	♢ Q 4	No	No		
♣ A K	♣ Q J 3	*For takeout			

The defence takes two diamonds and switches to a club. How do you handle the trumps? What would your answer be if the 3♢ opening had come from North?

(2)

WEST	EAST	WEST	NORTH	EAST	SOUTH
♠ K J 9 4 2	♠ A 10 5 3		3♣	Dble*	No
♡ 8	♡ K Q J 4	4♠	No	No	No
♢ K J 8 3	♢ A Q 9	*For takeout			
♣ J 7 2	♣ 8 3				

North leads ♣K, South winning with the ace. A heart goes to North's ace and North continues with the ♣Q (South discards a diamond) and ♣10. How must West play?

Solutions: (1) With no opposition bidding, you would have no basis for playing hearts in any but the normal way, ace and king and hope for the drop.

After a pre-empt, however, breaks are not normal and the pre-emptor tends to have little of significance outside the long suit. It makes sense therefore to play the pre-emptor's partner for the missing side strength.

Here, if South opened 3♢, you should place the ♡Q with North and play ♡A and then finesse the 10 if North plays low on the second round. North will hold ♡Q-x-x far more often than South will have ♡Q-x. Likewise, if North opened 3♢, you place the ♡Q with South and play ♡K followed by a finesse of the ♡J.

(2) In view of North's 3♣ pre-empt, you place the ♠Q with South. Further, North has shown up with ♡A and ♣K-Q, 9 points, making it wildly unlikely that North also has the ♠Q. You must not discard on the third club or ruff low in dummy—South's overruff will defeat you. Rise with the ♠A and lead the ♠10, running it if South plays low. Assuming the ♠10 holds, take a second spade finesse and claim.

TIP 72:

Do not follow any tip blindly—do not settle for probabilities if you can discover the location of key cards with certainty—make the opponents reveal what they have.

WEST	EAST	Neither side vulnerable.
♠ K 10 8 6 2	♠ A Q 9 3	
♡ 8 7	♡ J 10	
◇ 9	◇ K Q 8	
♣ K 10 9 7 4	♣ A J 6 3	

WEST	NORTH	EAST	SOUTH
	3♡	Dble*	4♡
4♠	No	No	No

*takeout

North leads ♡K and the second heart is won by South's ace. South switches to the 4 of spades, won by dummy's 9, North playing the 5. You play ♠A and a spade to your king, South following 7-J and North discarding two hearts. How do you continue?

Suppose you next play the ◇9 to dummy's king. South takes the ace and returns a diamond, dummy's queen capturing North's jack. What next?

It may seem tempting to tackle clubs after drawing trumps and, following Tip 71, place the ♣Q with South, so that ♣A and a club to the 10 is indicated. Even after a diamond to the king and ace and a diamond return from South, you may feel the urge to start the clubs.

Resist that urge—there is not the same rush in tackling a side suit as there would be if that suit were trumps. You may discover more information by playing the other suits first. It costs you nothing to ruff dummy's third diamond first and enlightenment may be close at hand.

Suppose that North discards another heart when you ruff the third diamond. You now know North started with *one* spade, *seven* hearts and *two* diamonds precisely. Hence North must have *three* clubs. Now the club play is a sure thing: cash the king and lead the 10, finessing against North, a play you would not have produced had you followed Tip 71 blindly. North held:

♠ 5 ♡ K Q 9 6 4 3 2 ◇ J 7 ♣ Q 8 2.

TIP 73:

Do not take a normal trump finesse if a ruff is threatened.

WEST	EAST	WEST	NORTH	EAST	SOUTH
♠ K J 5	♠ 10 6 4 3	1♡	Dble	2♡	No
♡ Q J 10 9 4	♡ A 6 3 2	4♡	No	No	No
◇ A	◇ 8 6				
♣ A Q 9 3	♣ K 8 7				

North leads ◇ K. Plan West's play.

The hand looks so easy. Win the ◇ A and lead the ♡ Q for a finesse. Even if the finesse loses, you should lose no more than one heart and two spades.

Just wait a minute! Reflect on the bidding for a moment. North doubled and is likely to hold the ♡ K but if not, North will hold all the remaining significant high cards including the A-Q in spades. North also appears to have four spades for the double and that leaves South with just two spades.

You can already foresee what will happen if South has something like ♠ 92 ♡ K8 ◇ 975432 ♣ 654. South would win the ♡ K, switch to the ♠ 9 and after ♠ Q and ♠ A, the third spade gives South a ruff. One off.

The correct move after the ◇ A is to lead the queen of hearts, tempting North to cover if holding the king. *Lead top of equal cards if you want a defender to cover your honour.* Do not let the queen run—you were never intending to finesse. Rise with the ♡ A and play a second heart. This will draw trumps if they are 2-2 and you avoid the spade ruff.

If South started with K-x-x in hearts, you have no way of escaping the spade ruff, but it is a shame to fail when South has just K-x.

TIP 74:

Form a habit of counting your winners even in a trump contract. This will often indicate what you need in order to succeed.

WEST	EAST		Dealer West: both vulnerable.		
♠ 2	♠ 8 7 6 5 3	WEST	NORTH	EAST	SOUTH
♡ K Q 10 9 6 4 3	♡ A J 8	3♡	No	4♡	No
◇ 8 2	◇ A 9	No	No		
♣ A 6 3	♣ 9 5 4				

North leads ♣Q. Plan the play.

Most players would win with the ♣A and tackle trumps, ending one off and venting their spleen on partner later for 'that maniacal raise'. This is a dangerous ploy if partner can retort 'You could have made it.'.

Count your winners: seven hearts and two aces. Where can the tenth trick come from? No ruffs in dummy, no high cards to establish. The only hope is the spade suit. You have to hope spades are 4-3 and you can set up the fifth spade for a diamond discard.

Win the ♣A and play a spade *at once*. You need all of those hearts in dummy for entries to ruff spades and to reach the ultimate spade winner. Suppose the North-South hands are:

NORTH
♠ A Q 10
♡ 7 2
◇ K 7 4 3
♣ Q J 10 8

SOUTH
♠ K J 9 4
♡ 5
◇ Q J 10 6 5
♣ K 7 2

North will win the spade, cash the ♣J and play a club to South. The ◇Q exit will be taken by dummy's ace. Now ruff a spade, heart to the 8, ruff a spade, heart to jack and ruff a spade. If spades are 4-3, dummy's last spade is high, heart to the ace, cash the fifth spade and away goes the diamond loser.

Note that even one round of trumps would have been fatal—you would be one entry short.

An ill-bred South might complain to North: 'A diamond lead will defeat it. Takes out an entry and we can lead a trump when a spade is led to knock out another entry'. That is quite correct, of course, even though unreasonable if suggesting North is blameworthy. You can feign sympathy for the defence as you bask in the glow of partner's congratulations on your fine play.

TIP 75:

If one opponent is marked with a shortage in one suit, place that opponent with the length in another critical suit. When missing an honour card in that critical suit, play the opponent known or expected to have the length to hold the missing honour.

WEST	EAST
♠ 5 3	♠ 10 7
♡ K 9 6 5	♡ A 2
◇ A K 9 5	◇ Q 10 3 2
♣ 8 6 2	♣ Q 10 9 5 3

Dealer East: North-South vulnerable.

WEST	NORTH	EAST	SOUTH
		No	1♣
No	1♠	No	2♠
No	No	2NT*	No
3◇	No	No	No

*Delayed takeout for the minors (see Tip 30)

North leads the ♣ J, queen, king. The ♣ A is cashed and South continues with the ♣ 7, ruffed by North. North switches to the ♠ K. ♠ 9 from South and a spade to South's ace. South continues with the ♣ 4. How should you play?

You are already one off, but that is the price for competing against their unassailable 2♠. No need to be two off if you can avoid it.

Your problem is whether to ruff high or with the 9 and this is where the tip comes in. North is known to be short in clubs and thus could have the length in diamonds. As the diamond length should be with North, the missing ◇ J is also likely to be with North. Therefore if you ruff with the ◇ 9, North will overruff with the ◇ J.

Best chance is to ruff with the ◇ A and then tackle trumps: ◇ K and a second diamond. If North began with something like: ♠ K Q 8 6 4, ♡ 10 8 7 3, ◇ J 8 6, ♣ J, the ◇ J will appear on the second round of trumps and the rest are yours.

If North follows low on the second round of diamonds, the better shot is to play the queen and assume North started with ◇ x-x-x and South with ◇ J-x. This is more likely than North holding ◇ J-x-x-x and South ◇ x, for with a singleton diamond, South is very likely to have pushed on to 3♠ and with four trumps and a singleton in partner's opening, North might have doubled 3◇.

TIP 76:

Be prepared to re-assess your plan of play if a surprising development occurs.

WEST	EAST	WEST	NORTH	EAST	SOUTH
♠ A K J 3 2	♠ 8 5 4	2♣(1)	No	2♦(2)	No
♡ A K 4 3	♡ Q 8 2	2♠	No	3♠	No
♦ 6 3	♦ A 5	4♣(3)	No	4♦(3)	No
♣ A K	♣ 8 7 4 3 2	6♠	No	No	No

(1) Artificial game-force
(2) Artificial negative
(3) Cue bids

West's slam jump was a little impetuous. We have all been in better slams but I daresay we have also been in worse. No point worrying about the bidding once the lead is made. You must direct your energies to bringing the slam home.

North leads ♦ K. Plan West's play.

West's thoughts might run swiftly on these lines: 'All will be well if trumps are 3-2 with the queen onside and hearts are 3-3. Actually if trumps are 3-2 and hearts 3-3, I do not need the ♠ Q onside. I can play ♠ A, ♠ K, cash the hearts and pitch the diamond from dummy on the thirteenth heart. The ♠ Q may ruff this but my diamond loser will be ruffed with dummy's last trump.'

A trump is led from dummy and South plays the queen! In theory, South's queen could be a falsecard from Q-x, but you should assume a key high honour from an opponent is a genuine card and here would be singleton. Not many defenders are good enough to find startling falsecards and the ♠ Q from Q-x here is not at all safe. West might hold ♠ A J 10 9 7 6 2 and the ♠ Q from Q-x would be an idiocy, crashing with partner's singleton king.

Once you place South with the ♠ Q bare, you must re-assess your plan. It will not do now to play ♠ A, ♠ K and run hearts. Even if they are 3-3, imagine North holds something like ♠ 10976 ♡965 ♦ K Q J 7 ♣ J 9—North would ruff the thirteenth heart and lead the last trump, eliminating dummy's trump and stranding you with a diamond loser.

Win the ♠ A, do not play a second trump but tackle the hearts at once. When they are 3-3 you lead the thirteenth heart and pitch dummy's diamond.

North may ruff this but you win any return, ruff your diamond loser, come to hand and draw North's trumps. Successful players are flexible declarers.

TIP 77:

If there is only one lie of the cards which will allow your contract to succeed, assume the cards lie that way.

WEST	EAST	Dealer East: Both vulnerable.
♠ 4 3	♠ Q 8 6 5	
♡ J 8 6 4 2	♡ K 10 5 3	
◇ K Q J 8	◇ A	
♣ K 2	♣ A Q 9 4	

WEST	NORTH	EAST	SOUTH
		1♣	1♠
2♡	No	4♡	No
No	No		

North leads ♠K followed by the ♠2, low, 10 from South. South continues with the ♠7. What should West do?

Clearly North is out of spades (South should have five spades for the overcall, North led the king of spades, and so on) so West ruffs with the jack of hearts. This wins the trick, North discarding a diamond. How should West continue?

If North could not overruff the ♡J, South will hold A-Q. Then you are doomed, no matter what. Forget that prospect—successful players are always optimists.

What genuine possibilities are there? North cannot have A-Q. North would overruff with the queen to ensure one down. In fact, North cannot hold the ♡Q at all, else North would overruff with the queen. The only hope is that North holds the ace and South has the queen.

Therefore you lead a heart at trick 4, 7 from North and play the king from dummy. Sure enough, South's queen drops and you concede just one trump trick to North who started with ♠K2 ♡A97 ◇109642 ♣863.

Note that North did well not to overruff your ♡J with the ace. Otherwise the location of the ♡Q would be transparent and the need to play the ♡K to drop the singleton queen would be even more obvious.

TIP 78:

Do not play for a competent opponent to make an elementary blunder.

WEST	EAST	WEST	NORTH	EAST	SOUTH
♠ K Q J 3 2	♠ A 10 8 6	1♠	No	3♣	No
♡ K 10 9 7	♡ A 6 3	3♡	No	3♠	No
◇ A 10	◇ K 2	4♠	No	4NT	No
♣ 8 5	♣ A Q 10 6	5◇	No	6♠	No
		No	No		

North leads ◇ 3. Plan the play. South has ♠ 9-5-4 and North the bare 7.

A heart loser seems inevitable and the slam seems to hinge on the club finesse. However, if South has Q-J-x in hearts or Q-x-x in hearts, you may be able to endplay South and avoid the need for the club finesse. If North has Q-x-x or Q-J-x in hearts, you can always fall back on the club finesse.

If West thinks on these lines, the play would go: win the diamond, draw the trumps in three rounds (North discards two diamonds), cash the other diamond and play ♡ A, heart to the king and exit with a heart. If South started with three hearts and wins the third heart, your worries are over.

Nice line? No—it is terrible. The fallacies are that a competent South would see the endplay coming and would jettison the Q from Q-x-x and even the Q and J from Q-J-x, so that South will make sure to avoid the endplay, and hearts may not be 3-3 at all.

In fact, North held ♠ 7, ♡ Q J 8 2, ◇ Q 7 4 3, ♣ K 4 3 2 and when declarer followed the above line, North won the third heart and played the fourth heart, stranding declarer in dummy to lead away from the ♣ A-Q-10-6!

Best play is win the ◇ A and draw trumps, followed by a finesse of the ♣ Q. If this wins, all is over. If South wins, declarer can win any return in dummy and may play for a club-heart squeeze. Give North the hand as above but with J-x-x-x in clubs and you can see that North must guard both hearts and clubs and will succumb to a squeeze.

TIP 79:

When running suits like K-Q-J-x opposite A-10-x-x, you can choose the order in which the winners are played, and may be able to force the opponent shorter in this suit to make two or more discards before receiving a useful signal from partner.

Dummy   A 10 7 2   or   A 10 7   or   A 10 7 4

Declarer   K Q J 8   K Q J 8 3   K Q J 8 3

When you have suits such as these, the order in which you play your winners will not matter to you. By making the opponent short in that suit play second repeatedly, you delay as long as possible any useful signal from partner. For example:

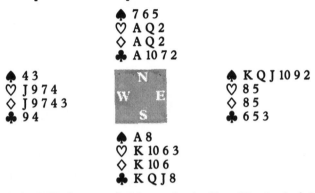

```
                    ♠ 7 6 5
                    ♡ A Q 2
                    ◇ A Q 2
                    ♣ A 10 7 2
   ♠ 4 3                              ♠ K Q J 10 9 2
   ♡ J 9 7 4          N               ♡ 8 5
   ◇ J 9 7 4 3    W        E          ◇ 8 5
   ♣ 9 4              S               ♣ 6 5 3
                    ♠ A 8
                    ♡ K 10 6 3
                    ◇ K 10 6
                    ♣ K Q J 8
```

South is in 6NT after a weak 2♠ opening by East. West leads ♠4 and South ducks East's spade but wins the spade continuation. The success of the contract hinges on declarer's making four heart tricks. West can prevent that but does not know South's exact pattern. South could just as easily hold four diamonds and three hearts.

South plays the clubs to give West the discarding problem: club to the ace, a club back to the king, ♣Q and ♣J. On the third club, West will discard a diamond but on the fourth club West must discard with J-9-7-4 in each red suit. If West knew South's 4-card red suit, West would know which one to keep and which to ditch. As West does not know, West will guess wrongly some of the time.

However, if declarer were to play ♣K, ♣Q, club to dummy and lead the fourth club from dummy, East could play either red 8 to show a doubleton. Then West could work out the red suit position and discard a diamond.

It is true that East could switch to a red 8 after holding the first trick but this could be an error if South held K 10 9 x in that red suit and West's jack would be trapped.

TIP 80:

When you have a choice of ways in which to play a key suit, do not commit yourself until you have studied all the inferences from the bidding, the lead and the play so far.

Dealer South:
North-South vulnerable

WEST	EAST	WEST	NORTH	EAST	SOUTH
♠ A Q 6 4	♠ 9 5 3				1♣
♡ 3	♡ 10 8 6 2				
◇ Q 10 9 8 6 4 3	◇ A	1◇	1♡	No	1NT*
♣ A	♣ J 8 7 6 2	3◇	3NT	No	No
		4◇	Dble	All pass	

*15-16 points

North leads ♣Q. Plan West's play.

West's 4◇ sacrifice turned out badly when the ◇A appeared in dummy. Perhaps East should have doubled 3NT, but it is no good worrying about that now. Success forgives all errors and if you make 4◇ doubled, there will be no recriminations.

You win the ♣A, cross to the ◇A (North plays the 2 and South the 7) and finesse the ♠Q which holds. How do you continue?

You have to lose a heart, a diamond and a spade. To make 4◇ doubled, you will have to avoid two diamond losers. If either opponent began with K-J-x, there is no hope, but if the honours are split you can hold your trump losers to one.

NORTH	J 2	NORTH	J 5 2
SOUTH	K 7 5	SOUTH	K 7

Lead the ◇Q and pin the jack. Lead low and drop the king, capturing the jack later.

Which situation exists? With this kind of problem, go over all the data so far and try to reconstruct the opponents' hands.

Spades: If you are to succeed, spades will have to be 3-3 else you will lose two spades. Assume therefore that spades are 3-3.

Hearts: South will not hold four hearts (would have raised) and North will not have six hearts (would have rebid 3♡ or 4♡, not 3NT). Thus, North will have five hearts and South three.

Clubs: North led the ♣Q with the jack in dummy, so that North should have started with Q-x in clubs, leaving South with five clubs.

North's pattern can be deduced to be 3-5-3-2 and South has 3-3-2-5. The ◇K will be with South for the 1NT bid, so that the winning move is a low diamond at trick four. South held:

♠ K J 2   ♡ K Q 4   ◇ K 7   ♣ K 10 5 4 3

TIP 81:

Keep track of the tricks needed to defeat the contract.

There is no point in pursuing a line of defence which has no chance of
success. Make a conscious mental note of the tricks you need to beat
declarer and you will frequently find the right path and avoid plays
doomed to failure.

(1) Dummy

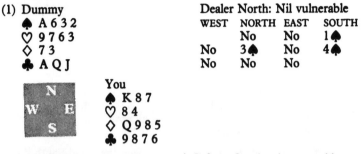

	WEST	NORTH	EAST	SOUTH
		No	No	1♠
	No	3♠	No	4♠
	No	No	No	

Dealer North: Nil vulnerable

Dummy
♠ A 6 3 2
♡ 9 7 6 3
◇ 7 3
♣ A Q J

You
♠ K 8 7
♡ 8 4
◇ Q 9 8 5
♣ 9 8 7 6

West leads ◇4: three, queen, ace. ♠Q from South, nine, two, king.
How should East continue?

(2) Dummy

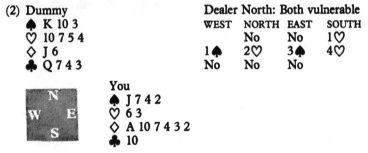

Dealer North: Both vulnerable

	WEST	NORTH	EAST	SOUTH
		No	No	1♡
	1♠	2♡	3♠	4♡
	No	No	No	

Dummy
♠ K 10 3
♡ 10 7 5 4
◇ J 6
♣ Q 7 4 3

You
♠ J 7 4 2
♡ 6 3
◇ A 10 7 4 3 2
♣ 10

West leads ◇5: six, ace, eight. How should East continue?

Solutions: (1) It is a sound principle to return partner's lead in general,
but it is important to check whether returning partner's lead can
produce the tricks needed to defeat the contract.

Here, if dummy were void in diamonds, East would not consider
bringing a diamond back. With a singleton left in dummy, a diamond
return is just as futile. East needs four tricks. One trick is in with the
♠K, and there is at most one more diamond trick. Where could the
defence take the other two tricks? A glance at dummy will confirm
there are no club tricks, so it must be the hearts and East should
switch to the 8 of hearts. If West holds: ♠9 ♡AQ52 ◇J10642
♣K53 East will score a heart ruff, while a diamond back allows
declarer to make in comfort.

If West holds: ♠9 ♡KQ52 ◇K10642 ♣1042 South began with ♠QJ1054 ♡AJ10 ◇AJ ♣K53 and the heart return is also vital to prevent a later endplay on West. If East brought back a diamond, West would win but could not afford to lead a heart. West could exit safely only with a club, South would win, draw trumps, eliminate clubs and lead a heart to the 10, endplaying West. On a heart return, ducked to West, West would win ♡Q, cash ◇K and exit with a club and await the ♡K in due course to set the contract.

(2) It is encouraging to all of us that in the 1981 World Championships, East muffed the defence when he won the ◇A and returned a diamond. Had East paid attention to the tricks needed to defeat the contract, the futility of the diamond return would have been recognised.

Four tricks are needed. ◇A is one and at most there will be one spade trick and one more diamond trick. If a trump trick is coming, it will come in good time. If there is no trump trick, a club trick is vital and East should switch to the ♣10 at trick 2.

As it happened, the club switch can defeat the contract by two tricks. West held: ♠AQ985 ♡Q2 ◇Q95 ♣A92. The successful defence: club to the ace, nine of clubs ruffed, spade to ace, another club ruff. On the actual diamond return, South won with the king.

South: ♠6 ♡AKJ98 ◇K8 ♣KJ865.

Next came ♡A, ♡K and South lost only the three missing aces.

There is a sacrifice available in 4♠ (doubled, one off), but why sacrifice in 4♠ when you can defeat their game by competent defence?

TIP 82:

Stop and count the cards in a suit after two rounds of the suit have been played.

After two rounds of a suit you can frequently tell what is happening in that suit. Noting the order in which partner played the cards (high-low = even number) together with the cards in dummy and those left in your hand will give you the picture of what is happening.

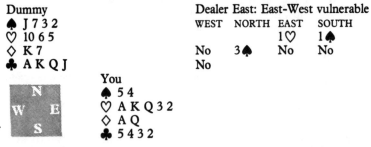

Dummy
- ♠ J 7 3 2
- ♡ 10 6 5
- ◇ K 7
- ♣ A K Q J

Dealer East: East-West vulnerable

WEST	NORTH	EAST	SOUTH
		1♡	1♠
No	3♠	No	No
No			

You
- ♠ 5 4
- ♡ A K Q 3 2
- ◇ A Q
- ♣ 5 4 3 2

West leads ♡8: five-queen-nine from declarer. On the king of hearts, South plays the jack and West the seven. How should East continue?

In 9 out of 10 average games, East would continue with the ♡A. West would discard a club or a diamond and 3♠ would make easily on a layout like this:

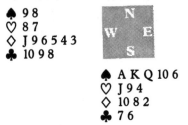

- ♠ 9 8
- ♡ 8 7
- ◇ J 9 6 5 4 3
- ♣ 10 9 8

- ♠ A K Q 10 6
- ♡ J 9 4
- ◇ 10 8 2
- ♣ 7 6

After the second round of hearts, East notes West's 8-7, high-low, and knows South has another heart. The temptation to cash the third heart is almost irresistible. If East notes Tip 81 ('Keep track of the tricks needed to defeat the contract'), East will note that three hearts and the ◇A are not enough. East needs two diamond tricks and for that West has to obtain the lead.

The solution is easy once East has counted the hearts after two rounds. West is now out of hearts, so East leads a low heart, forcing West to ruff. West makes the obvious diamond return, one off.

It is true that if East plays the ♡A at trick 3, West should ruff this and switch to diamonds. However, in real life an average defender does not ruff partner's winners and East should ensure West does the right thing. We all know Murphy's First Law of Defence: If you give partner the chance to do the wrong thing, partner grabs that chance.

TIP 83:

A high card from partner playing third-hand-high denies the card immediately below it.

A general principle for the defenders is to win a trick as cheaply as possible. A corollary of the same rule is that when playing third-hand-high, you play the cheapest of equally high cards. This makes it easier for partner to calculate the cards held by you and by declarer. If third-hand-high plays the cheapest of equally high cards, it follows that the card played by third hand denies the card immediately below it (as that would then be an equal and cheaper card).

Examples:

	NORTH
	Dummy
WEST	7 5
J 8 6 4 2	

West leads the 4 and East plays the 10, taken by the ace. West can tell that South started with A-K-Q-9 (the K and Q as East would have played the K or Q, third hand high). South has the 9 as East's 10 denies the 9. With 10-9, East should have played the 9.

	NORTH
	Dummy
WEST	7 5
Q 8 6 4 2	

West leads the 4. If East plays the 10 taken by South's ace, West can continue the suit as East has the jack. If East plays the jack taken by South's ace, West knows that South has A-K-10 (East's J denied the 10) and therefore the suit must not be continued by West.

	NORTH
	Dummy
WEST	7 5
K 9 6 4 2	

West leads the 4. If East plays the jack taken by the ace, West knows that East has the queen and South has the 10 (the jack denied the 10) and it is safe to play a low card later to East's queen. If East had played the queen, taken by the ace, West would know that South held the jack (denied by East's queen) and it would be an error to lead a low card later. West should cash the king or switch to another suit to try to give East the lead to play through South's jack.

TIP 84:

Do not play third hand high if it will benefit only declarer.

In a trump contract partner will not lead a low card when holding the ace in the suit led. Knowing that declarer holds the ace may enable third player to calculate that playing high in third seat cannot win the trick and will only build up winners for declarer or dummy. In such cases, withhold your honour—there is no merit in playing a high card if it benefits only declarer.

Examples:

(1)	NORTH		Dummy plays the jack on
	K J 10 9 8	EAST	West's 5.
West leads the 5		Q 7 6 3 2	What should East do?

(2)	NORTH		Dummy plays the queen on
	Q J 10 7	EAST	West's 8.
8 led		K 6 4 3	What should East do?

(3)	NORTH		Dummy plays the ten on
	K 10 9 6 3	EAST	West's 8.
8 led		J 5 4 2	What should East do?

Solutions: (1) The situation could be either of these:

```
     K J 10 9 8          or        K J 10 9 8
5                Q 7 6 3 2   5 4                Q 7 6 3 2
     A 4                          A
```

If East plays the queen on dummy's jack, South has five tricks in this suit whichever position exists. If East correctly plays low, declarer can score only four tricks.

(2) The situation could be any of these:

```
(a)    Q J 10 7             (b)    Q J 10 7
8 5              K 6 4 3     9 8 5            K 6 4 3
       A 9 2                        A 2
```

```
(c)    Q J 10 7
8                K 6 4 3
       A 9 5 2
```

If East plays the king on dummy's queen, declarer has four tricks in each case. If East correctly plays low, declarer has at most three tricks in (a) and (b), and in (c) declarer was entitled to four tricks anyway.

(3) The situations could be:

```
(a)    K 10 9 6 3          (b)    K 10 9 6 3
8 7              J 5 4 2    8                J 5 4 2
       A Q                         A Q 7
```

If East plays the jack on dummy's 10, South has five tricks in (a) and (b). If East correctly plays low, South has at most 4 tricks with (a), while with (b), South always had five tricks once partner led the 8. By playing low, East at least blocks the suit.

110

TIP 85:

Do not cover an honour with an honour if partner is short in the suit led and you have no clearcut card to be promoted.

The purpose of covering an honour with an honour is to win the trick or build up a trick for your side. If your side has no chance of benefiting, it is foolish to cover the honour. If you have no card that could be promoted by a cover, then it will help to cover only if partner has a significant, promotable card. If partner has at most two cards in the suit, then that possibility ceases to exist.

(1) NORTH   If this is the trump suit and the
    Dummy   queen is led, should East cover?
    Q 6 4 2   EAST
              K 7 5   East has no secondary card to
                         promote and West figures to have
only one or two cards. It cannot gain to cover, so East should play low smoothly.

Can it cost to cover? You better believe it.

        Q 6 4 2   If the situation is like this, then
A   K 7 5   South will be chortling all the
        J 10 9 8 3   way to the bank as your king
                         telescopes the defence's two tricks
                         into one.

Some players wrongly argue that they are hoping to promote partner's jack. You cannot make more than one trick if partner does have the jack no matter how you play.

        Q 6 4 2   If East covers the Q in this
J 8   K 7 5   position, West wins the jack, but
        A 10 9 3   if East plays low, the defence still
                         wins one trick later.

        NORTH
        Dummy   If this is the trump suit and the
        J 7 5 4 2   EAST   jack is led, should East cover?
               Q 6   Again East has no secondary card
and West must be short in the suit. East must play low. Imagine East's chagrin (and West's unprintable comments) if West held the bare king! If East plays low smoothly, declarer with K 10 9 8 3 may misguess and play the king, giving East a trick with the queen, a trick that could not eventuate if East covered the jack.

TIP 86:

Third hand plays the lower honour when holding an 'almost surround' combination over dummy's honour.

Third-hand-high is vital when dummy has only low cards. With an honour card in dummy, that situation may change. These situations are obvious:

	(1) Dummy		(2) Dummy	
West leads the 4	K 6 5	EAST	Q 6 5	EAST
Dummy plays low		A Q 3		K J 3
	(3) Dummy			
	J 6 5	EAST		
		Q 10 3		

(1) East plays the queen (2) East plays the jack (3) East plays the 10.

In each case East has a perfect surround of dummy's honour. A 'near-surround' exists when the higher or the lower honour with East is one or two cards away from the perfect surround.

In each of the following examples West leads the 4, dummy plays low. What should East play?

(4) Dummy		(5) Dummy		(6) Dummy	
K 6 5	EAST	K 6 5	EAST	K 6 5	EAST
	A J 3		A 10 3		A 8 3

(4) East should play the jack, not the ace.
(5) East should usually play the 10 and keep the ace to capture the king later.
(6) East should play the ace. The low card is too low to count as a near surround.

(7) Dummy		(8) Dummy		(9) Dummy	
Q 6 5	EAST	Q 6 5	EAST	Q 6 5	EAST
	A J 3		K 10 3		A J 10

(7) East should play the jack, not the ace.
(8) East should play the 10, not the king.
(9) East should play the 10. When playing the lower of the surround cards, you play the cheapest of equals in third seat (see Tip 83).

(10) Dummy		(11) Dummy		(12) Dummy	
A J 5	EAST	A J 5	EAST	A 10 5	EAST
	K 10 3		Q 9 3		Q 9 3

(10) East should play the 10, not the king.
(11) East should play the 9, not the queen.
(12) East should play the 9, not the queen.

The above are the general technical guidelines. On a particular hand you may judge it is correct to depart from the normal technique.

TIP 87:

Lead top of the 'imaginary sequence' when you sit over dummy and a surround position exists.

Study these positions:

(1)	J 6 5		(2)	10 4 3	
8 7 4		A Q 10 3	7 6 2		K J 9 8
	K 9 2			A Q 5	

(3)	10 4 3	
A 7 6		K J 9 8
	Q 5 2	

(1) If East leads the 3, declarer has two tricks by playing low. If East leads the queen—South's king winning—and East waits for West to lead the suit next, South makes just one trick.

(2) If East leads the 8, declarer has three tricks by playing low and letting the 10 win. If East leads the jack, declarer can be held to two tricks if East waits for West to lead the suit next.

(3) If East leads the 8, declarer makes one trick by playing low. If East leads the jack, declarer makes no tricks.

The common features of these positions are:

(a) The defender is sitting *over* dummy and
(b) The defender has dummy's high card surrounded (the card above it and the card below it), and
(c) The defender has another higher honour.

In these cases, imagine dummy's high card is in the defender's hand and make the standard lead from that holding. Thus, in (1) East imagines holding A Q J 10 3 and leads the queen, while in (2) and (3) East visualises K J 10 9 8 and leads the jack, top of the 'imaginary sequence'.

What card should East lead in these positions, if intending to attack this suit?

(4)	9 7 4		(5)	9 7 4	
5 3		Q 10 8 6	K 5 3		Q 10 8 6
	A K J 2			A J 2	

(6)	A 9 4	
K 5 3		Q 10 8 6
	J 7 2	

East has dummy's 9 *surrounded* in each case, visualises the 9 in hand, making Q-10-9-8-6 and leads the 10 in each case, top of the imagined sequence. In (4), a low card allows South four tricks; the 10 limits South to three. In (5) and (6), a low card enables South to win two tricks by playing low, while the 10 holds South to one trick only.

TIP 88:

If partner plays the cards in an abnormal order, partner is sending you a message, usually a suit-preference signal.

This position is standard:

♠ A 9 6 3
♡ K J 5
◇ 9 5 2
♣ 10 6 5

♠ 8
♡ A 8 6 4 3
◇ J 10 7 6 3
♣ J 2

South opens 1♠ and rebids 4♠ over North's 2♠ raise. West leads the ◇6, East winning with the ace. East continues with ◇K. What should West play?

East's sequence of plays must make an impact on West, as East has not played the diamonds in normal order. A defender wins a trick as cheaply as possible (see Tip 83) but East played ace-then-king, whereas king first would be normal. The message here is that East has A-K doubleton and East now needs to know West's entry.

West should drop the ◇J under the king, high-card for the high suit, asking for a heart switch. East started with ♠754 ♡972 ◇AK ♣98743. Without West's ◇J signal for hearts, East would surely switch to clubs, dummy's weakness, and declarer makes easily. On the heart switch, West wins and gives East the diamond ruff for one down.

♠ A K 8 2
♡ Q J 5 3
◇ 9 5 2
♣ K 9

WEST	NORTH	EAST	SOUTH
		1◇	Dble
No	2◇	Dble	2♡
No	4♡	No	No
No			

♠ 9 7 6 5 3
♡ 9 2
◇ 8 6
♣ 8 6 5 4

West leads ◇8 and East wins the ace, South playing the 10. East continues with ◇K, South playing the jack. Next comes ◇7, ◇4 from South and West ruffs. How should West continue?

An alert West would spot East's abnormal play in diamonds. Normal would be to win with the cheapest card possible, yet East played ace first, king next—there is no doubleton possibility here, so what does ace-then-king mean? The abnormal order is usually a suit-preference signal. Partner played the highest diamond first and next the highest diamond left. Partner's signal is for the high suit. West should lead a spade, since East began with ♠— ♡876 ◇AKQ73 ♣QJ732 and East had no other way to draw West's attention to the necessity of the spade shift for the killing ruff. If West returns a club or a heart, declarer wins the rest.

TIP 89:

Keep length with dummy.

When dummy has four cards in a suit and you also hold four cards, you should not discard from that suit if you could win a trick. If dummy holds five cards in a suit and you hold four or five cards, again you should retain your length if you could win a trick.

Examples:

(1)	A Q 6 4		(2)	K Q 7 4 2	
J 10 8		9 7 3 2	J 8		9 6 5 3
	K 5			A 10	

(1) South has three winners. If East discards a card, dummy's last card becomes high and declarer has a fourth trick.

(2) South has three winners and can set up a fourth trick if dummy has an entry. If East discards a card, declarer has five winners straight off without needing an outside entry in dummy.

		WEST	NORTH	EAST	SOUTH
♠ A 5				No	1NT*
♡ 8 7 2					
◇ A 10 6 5		No	3NT	All pass	
♣ A 8 7 4		*16–18 points			

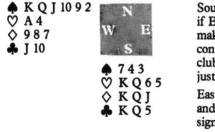

♠ 8 6
♡ J 10 9 3
◇ 4 3 2
♣ 9 6 3 2

West leads ♠ K, ducked in dummy and continues with the ♠ Q, taken by the ace. A diamond is led to declarer's king, the ◇ Q follows and the ◇ J is overtaken by dummy's ace. West following with the nine, eight, seven in that order. The ◇ 10 is led from dummy. What should East discard, a heart or a club?

On general grounds East should throw a heart and keep the *four* clubs because dummy has four clubs. The remaining cards are:

♠ K Q J 10 9 2
♡ A 4
◇ 9 8 7
♣ J 10

♠ 7 4 3
♡ K Q 6 5
◇ K Q J
♣ K Q 5

South has already five tricks and if East lets a club go, South can make four club tricks and the contract. If East keeps all four clubs, declarer has to settle for just eight tricks.

East should also keep the clubs and let a heart go since West has signalled strength in hearts in two ways. What were they?

On the second round of spades, West led the *queen*, an unnecessarily high card (it would be normal to knock out dummy's ace with a low card) and played the 9-8-7 of diamonds in abnormal order, highest followed by next highest (the normal order would be 7, then 8, then 9, low to high with an odd number). Both these abnormal plays indicate values in the high outside suit, hearts (see Tip 88).

TIP 90:

Keep length with declarer.

Just as it is vital to retain length in dummy's suit to prevent extra tricks being established, so it is imperative to retain length in a suit held by declarer. This is tougher since declarer's hand is not visible but the bidding frequently reveals what declarer would rather keep hidden. Pay attention to the bidding and your discarding problems may be simplified.

```
         ♠ K 7 5
         ♡ Q 3
         ◇ A 9 3
         ♣ A 9 7 5 4
♠ 8          ┌─────────┐
♡ 10 8 6 4 2 │    N    │
◇ Q J 10 7 2 │  W   E  │
♣ Q 6        │    S    │
             └─────────┘
```

WEST	NORTH	EAST	SOUTH
No	1♣	No	1♠
No	1NT	No	3♡
No	3♠	No	4NT(1)
No	5♣(2)	No	5♠(3)
No	5NT(4)	No	6♠
No	No	No	

(1) Roman Key Card Blackwood
(2) 0 or 3 key cards
(3) Sign-off in case it is 0 key cards
(4) 3 key cards, denies the trump queen

West leads ◇ Q: three, six, king. Declarer cashes the ♠ A and leads a spade to the king, West discards . . .? A spade from dummy: nine, ten and West discards . . .? Declarer now plays the ♠ Q. What should West discard now?

The first two discards are easy as two diamonds can be spared. On the third spade, West cannot afford another diamond as dummy's ◇ 9 would set up as a winner.

Most defenders would pitch a low heart but this is an error. The correct discard is the ♣ 6. The South hand is: ♠ A Q 10 4 2 ♡ A K 9 7 5 ◇ K ♣ J 3.

Following the 'keep length with declarer' tip, West will retain the hearts as declarer bid 3♡. If West pitches a heart, declarer gives up one heart and makes when the fifth heart is established. If West discards the ♣ 6, South can still make 6♡ double dummy but would not succeed in practice.

Another way to find the ♣ 6 discard is to reason that South's bidding reveals 5 spades—4 hearts at least, leaving at most four minor cards. If South holds ♣ K, South has no minor loser anyway, so that West must play East for the ♣ K.

TIP 91:

Make a mental note of declarer's likely shape during the bidding.

On most occasions the opponents will give away significant information about their holdings. Instead of sitting quietly bemoaning the fact that you have a rotten hand, forget your self-pity and spend the spare time during the auction fruitfully by estimating declarer's likely hand pattern. Continue this assessment when dummy appears and many defensive opportunities will become crystal clear.

(1)

♠ A 5 2
♡ K J 10 7 4
◇ 7 3
♣ A J 6

♠ Q 10 8 7
♡ A 9 2
◇ 10
♣ Q 9 8 7 4

WEST	NORTH	EAST	SOUTH
No	1♡	No	2◇
No	2♡	No	2♠
No	2NT	No	3♠
No	4♠	No	No
No			

West leads the ♣7, won by the ace, East playing the 5 and South the 2. The ◇3 is led to South's ace and South continues with the ♡8. Should West play the ace or play low?

(2)
♠ 8 3
♡ J 10 8 5
◇ J 10 3
♣ J 4 3 2

♠ 10 7 6 5 4 2
♡ 9
◇ Q 9 6
♣ A K 7

WEST	NORTH	EAST	SOUTH
	No	No	2♣(1)
No	2◇(2)	No	2♠
No	2NT	No	3♡
No	4♡	No	No
No			

(1) Game-force
(2) Negative

West leads the ♣10. How should East plan the defence?

Solutions: (1) South's bidding has revealed a 6-5 pattern, 5 spades as they were rebid and therefore six diamonds since they were bid ahead of spades and so must be a longer suit. With a 5-5 pattern, the spades would have been bid first.

South's club at trick one accounts for 12 cards and therefore South's heart is a singleton. This is no time to play low smoothly since South has no guess in hearts. The ♡K will be played and your ♡A will go begging. Grab the ace of hearts and play a second club. If South is no better than ♠KJ964 ♡8 ◇AKQ654 ♣2, you are well on the way to defeating the contract. If you duck, declarer can cope easily.

(2) South's 2♠ rebid showed five spades. Add your six spades to

dummy's doubleton and partner's void is transparent. Win ♣K and give partner the spade ruff, recapture the lead (hopefully) with ♣A and another spade ruff cooks declarer's goose. South's hand: ♠AKQJ9 ♡ AKQ76 ◇A ♣Q5.

Clearly you must not cash the second club before giving partner a spade ruff, otherwise you have no entry to give partner the second spade ruff needed to beat the contract.

TIP 92:

Make a mental note of declarer's likely point count during the bidding. As soon as dummy appears, count dummy's points.

Dummy's points are revealed at trick one. Add your points to dummy's and add opener's likely point range. Deduct this from 40 and partner's range of points becomes known. Often this will help you to calculate the defensive chances. For example, if partner's possible range is 4-6 points and partner has already shown an ace, it is futile to defend in the hope that partner could have an additional ace or a king.

♠ Q J 10 5
♡ Q J 10 5
◇ A 7
♣ J 6 2

WEST	NORTH	EAST	SOUTH
			1NT*
No	2♣	Dble	2♡
No	4♡	No	No
No			

♠ 8
♡ K 7 6 2
◇ Q J 8
♣ A K Q 10 4

*Weak. 12-14 points

West leads the ♣8: 2, 10, 5. ♣K from East: 9, 7 from West. How should East continue?

Without looking back at the problem, how many points are in dummy? If you do not have the answer at your fingertips, you are not using one of the best defensive clues. Dummy has 11 points, East began with 15 and South with 12-14. That is a total of 38-40 points, so partner's range is 0-2 points. Partner's 8-7 in clubs means another club trick is available but it would be foolish to cash the third club and lead the ♠8 . . . partner cannot hold the ♠K or ♠A.

A little closer examination of dummy and your hand reveals that all the queens and jacks are visible, so that partner cannot hold 1 or 2 points. So partner has no points and declarer has ♠AK ♡A ◇K.

Your only hope is that partner has the ♡8 or ♡9. You cash the third club and lead another club. If declarer holds, say, ♠AK6 ♡A943 ◇K52 ♣953 partner's ♡8 can force dummy's 10 (it does not help South to ruff with the 9) and if you cover either of dummy's remaining honours, you guarantee yourself a trump trick to set the contract.

TIP 93:

Clarify the defence for partner whenever possible.

On many occasions one partner knows how the defence should go while the other may be in the dark or have to guess. Murphy's Second Law of Defence: If partner has a guess in the defence, partner will guess wrongly. Your duty, then, if you know how the defence should proceed is to leave partner in no doubt.

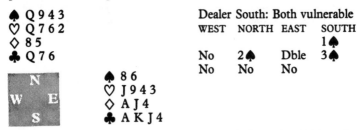

♠ Q 9 4 3
♡ Q 7 6 2
◇ 8 5
♣ Q 7 6

♠ 8 6
♡ J 9 4 3
◇ A J 4
♣ A K J 4

Dealer South: Both vulnerable

WEST	NORTH	EAST	SOUTH
			1♠
No	2♠	Dble	3♠
No	No	No	

West leads ◇ K. What card should East play? How should East plan the defence?

Recognising the defence needs five tricks (Tip 81), East calculates that as there are only two diamond tricks for the defence, three club tricks are necessary. While the need for a club switch is clear to East, West may have no inkling where the tricks are coming from. Suppose the missing hands are:

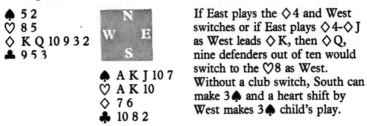

♠ 5 2
♡ 8 5
◇ K Q 10 9 3 2
♣ 9 5 3

♠ A K J 10 7
♡ A K 10
◇ 7 6
♣ 10 8 2

If East plays the ◇ 4 and West switches or if East plays ◇ 4-◇ J as West leads ◇ K, then ◇ Q, nine defenders out of ten would switch to the ♡ 8 as West. Without a club switch, South can make 3♠ and a heart shift by West makes 3♠ child's play.

It is no good East remonstrating with West after the hand is over. *Nobody wins a post mortem.* (Incidentally, a post mortem should seek only to fix the mistake, never to fix the blame.)

East's correct play is to overtake the ◇ K with the ace, *cash the king of clubs* to show partner where the tricks are, and return the ◇ 4 to West for the club return and five tricks for the defence.

Could the ◇ K be singleton or doubleton? Out of the question. If you suspect a singleton or doubleton lead, ask yourself what that would give declarer? If the ◇ K is doubleton or singleton, South would have six or seven diamonds, impossible on the bidding.

TIP 94:

Take control of the defence if you know what to do and partner may not be sure.

This is similar to the previous tip but Tip 93 operates when partner needs to be involved in the defence. Often partner does not have to be told anything and you know where the tricks have to be developed.

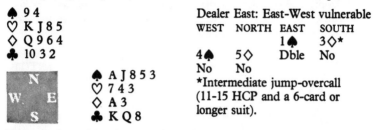

♠ 9 4
♡ K J 8 5
♢ Q 9 6 4
♣ 10 3 2

♠ A J 8 5 3
♡ 7 4 3
♢ A 3
♣ K Q 8

Dealer East: East-West vulnerable

WEST	NORTH	EAST	SOUTH
		1♠	3♢*
4♠	5♢	Dble	No
No	No		

*Intermediate jump-overcall (11-15 HCP and a 6-card or longer suit).

With a balanced hand, better for defence, and a trump trick, East elects to double rather than bid a risky 5♠.

West leads ♠K. Which card should East play? How should East plan the defence?

Observing Tip 81, East notes three tricks are needed. The likely tricks are one or two spades, one diamond and one club. If there is no second spade trick (South may have a singleton) the club trick is vital. East knows that, while West may not. Therefore East should take control of the defence: overtake the ♠K with the ace and switch to ♣K. This is vital on the actual deal as the missing hands are:

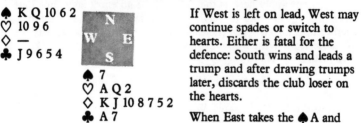

♠ K Q 10 6 2
♡ 10 9 6
♢ —
♣ J 9 6 5 4

♠ 7
♡ A Q 2
♢ K J 10 8 7 5 2
♣ A 7

If West is left on lead, West may continue spades or switch to hearts. Either is fatal for the defence: South wins and leads a trump and after drawing trumps later, discards the club loser on the hearts.

When East takes the ♠A and switches to ♣K, declarer can no longer succeed.

Corollary: If you are not sure how to continue, do *not* take control of the defence. For example, do not overtake partner's card unnecessarily if you are not sure what to do next, or if declarer leads low towards rags in dummy, do not play a highish card to win the trick if you cannot tell how to continue to best effect.

TIP 95:

If partner starts discarding from a suit led initially, do not return that suit.

When partner has found a good lead partner will want the suit returned and in such a case partner would not discard from that suit. However, partner may have found a poor lead and to make you aware that the original suit was not the best choice, partner will start discarding from that suit. Particularly at no-trumps, one tends not to discard from a suit you wish partner to lead.

♠ 9 3
♡ 8 7 2
♢ K 7 5
♣ K Q 5 4 2

	WEST	NORTH	EAST	SOUTH
				1NT(1)
	No	No	No	1NT(1)
	No	2NT	No	3NT
	No	No	No	
	(1) 16-18			

♠ 10 8 6
♡ J 4 3
♢ 9 8 6 3
♣ A 8 3

West leads the ♠4: nine, ten, king from declarer. South leads ♣J, West playing the 7. Plan East's defence.

East should duck this club and also a club continuation. West shows out on the second club. What should East do on winning the third club?

A defender with A-x or A-x-x should normally duck when declarer is seeking to establish a long suit in dummy if dummy is short of entries. This does not apply here as the ♢K will be an entry later, but East ducks in clubs in order to obtain a signal from West. East cannot tell whether to return a spade (normal) or a heart (occasionally) without assistance from West who may hold: ♠AJ542 ♡Q1095 ♢QJ2 ♣7 or ♠J7542 ♡AQ109 ♢QJ2 ♣7.

With the former, West would discard ♡5 then ♡9 in standard methods and a spade return would defeat the game (while a heart switch would let 3NT make). With the latter, West should discard ♠J and ♠7, denying any further interest in spades. East should then find the heart switch and lead the ♡J, not the standard low one. As four heart tricks seem vital, the ♡J is necessary any time West holds A-Q-10-x, while a low card allows South to duck and avoid four quick heart losers.

Using Suit-Preference Discards, West would discard the ♡10 first on the first hand and still the ♠J on the second, the high discard for the high suit in each case.

TIP 96:

Switch to lowest card = return this suit. Switch to high spot card = no interest in this suit.

♠ 5 3
♡ 7 4 2
◇ A K 10
♣ Q 10 7 5 2

WEST	NORTH	EAST	SOUTH
	No	No	1NT*
No	3NT	No	No
No			

*16–18

♠ 10 7 2
♡ A 10 5
◇ 9 6 4 3 2
♣ 8 6

West leads ♠6 and East's 10 is taken by the jack. South leads ♣K, 3 from West, 8 from East and ♣J is won by West's ace. West switches to a heart taken by the ace. How should East continue?

The answer is that East does not know how to continue without considering the actual heart led. If West led the ♡9, East should win the ♡A and return ♠7 (return top from a remaining doubleton). West will have something like: ♠AQ864 ♡9863 ◇75 ♣A3 and the spade return will defeat the contract. With this holding, West knows from East's ♠10 that South has at least K-9 left (see Tip 83) so that it is vital to put East on lead for a spade lead through South. West chooses the *nine* of hearts to deny interest in a heart return.

If West led the *three* of hearts, East should win the ♡A and return the *ten* of hearts (top from remaining doubleton). West will have something like ♠Q9864 ♡KJ93 ◇75 ♣A3 and the heart return is vital to beat 3NT. With this holding, West knows at trick one that South holds ♠AKJ and that the spades are useless. Therefore on winning the ♣A, West switches to hearts and chooses the *three*, the lowest, to ask for a heart return. East must co-operate, for a spade return would give declarer ten tricks.

TIP 97:

Obey partner's signals.

The function of most signalling is to let partner know what to do. Except for mechanical count signals which indicate the number of cards in a suit, signals usually indicate the direction in which the defence should go. A discouraging signal asks you not to continue the suit led: an encouraging signal requests the suit led to be continued. A suit-preference signal indicates the suit to which to switch.

When partner gives you an attitude signal or a suit-preference signal, you need justification 'beyond reasonable doubt' to act contrary to partner's signal. Even if partner's request seems abnormal, trust a competent partner, not the opposition. A good approach is the Post-Mortem Test: 'If I do not heed my partner's signal, will my partner/team-mates agree with my assessment later if it is wrong?' If you have any doubt, obey your partner.

	♠ K 9	Dealer North: Both vulnerable

		WEST	NORTH	EAST	SOUTH
	♠ K 9				
	♡ Q J 9	No	1NT*	No	4♠
	◊ A K J 8	No	No	No	
	♣ K J 10 7	*16–18 points			

♠ 7 2	
♡ A 8 7 6 2	
◊ 9 7 6 5 3	
♣ Q	

West leads ♣Q: king, ace, 4 from declarer. East returns ♣2, ruffed by West. How should West continue?

East has requested a diamond switch with the *two* of clubs (low card = low suit when giving a ruff or hoping partner will ruff). A diamond switch seems foolish looking at dummy and if your partner has never heard of a suit-preference signal, you may look elsewhere (preferably for a better partner). But if partner is competent and attentive, you ignore the diamond request at your peril. Imagine you decide to cash ♡A first, just in case, and the missing hands look like this:

	♠ 10 6 3
	♡ K 10 5 4 3
	◊ —
	♣ A 9 6 3 2

♠ A Q J 8 5 4
♡ —
◊ Q 10 4 2
♣ 8 5 4

South ruffs the ♡A and makes eleven tricks! How can you face partner as you realise that the diamond switch *as requested* would have led to two down? If partner has given the wrong signal, it will still be better for the future . . . partner will know you are paying attention and that you trust the signalling implicitly.

TIP 98:

The queen-signal by partner under your ace or king lead is either a singleton or promises the jack.

When discarding, an honour card signal promises the honours below and denies the honour above. Thus, a discard of an ace promises the king-queen, while the discard of a king promises the queen-jack and denies the ace. Likewise, the discard of a queen promises the jack-ten and denies the king.

When following suit to partner's king or ace lead, the play of the queen has a similar function.

Your queen-signal under the ace or king is very valuable because by confirming the jack or a singleton it means that it is safe for partner to lead a low card next—you guarantee that you will win the trick. It follows that you must not drop the queen from Q-doubleton (unless the second card is the jack).

	WEST	NORTH	EAST	SOUTH
♠ K 10 6 3				1♠
♡ A Q J 6		No	No	
◇ 7 3 2	Dble	2NT(1)	No	4♠
♣ J 7	No	No	No	

♠ 8 7
♡ 10 9 7 3
◇ A K 8
♣ A Q 8 3

(1) High card raise to 3♠ (Truscott Convention). 2NT over a double shows 10 HCP or more and support for opener. A direct raise to 3♠ over the double would be weaker and pre-emptive, 6-9 points and 8 losers. West leads ◇ K and East plays the queen. How should West continue?

West wants to have East on lead to bring a club through declarer into West's A-Q. The missing hands could be:

♠ 4
♡ 5 4 2
◇ Q J 10 6 4
♣ 9 5 4 2

♠ A Q J 9 5 2
♡ K 8
◇ 9 5
♣ K 10 6

When West leads ◇ 8, East easily finds the club switch for one down. If West plays ◇ K, then ◇ A, South makes 4♠ by discarding two clubs on the hearts after trumps are drawn.

♠ 10 9
♡ J 10 8 6
♦ A J 5
♣ A K J 6

WEST	NORTH	EAST	SOUTH
1♠	Dble	No	2♠
No	3♣	No	3♡
No	4♡	No	No
No			

♠ A K J 8 5 4
♡ A 7
♦ 8 6 3 2
♣ 8

West leads ♠K and East drops ♠Q. How should West continue?

West can count two spade tricks and the ♡A (Tip 81). How will a fourth trick materialise? Partner's queen-signal here must be a singleton as West holds the jack. Thus, partner can ruff a spade, but there is no hurry. Lead your singleton club, take the ♡A on the first lead of trumps and lead the ♠4 (low card asks for the low suit return when giving a ruff). East ruffs and your club ruff beats the contract. The missing hands are:

♠ Q
♡ 4 3 2
♦ 10 9 7 4
♣ 9 5 4 3 2

♠ 7 6 3 2
♡ K Q 9 5
♦ K Q
♣ Q 10 7

If West plays a second spade at trick 2, 4♡ succeeds.

TIP 99:

Watch partner's spot cards for secondary signals.

Often a defender will have spare cards after giving an initial signal. For example, if you give a count signal with the 2 from 952 to show an odd number, you can play the 5 or the 9 next. In such cases the normal order is 2-5-9. If you depart from the normal order, you are usually giving a suit-preference signal (see Tip 88). If you play the 9 on the second round, this would be a suit-preference for the higher suit. If you play the 5 second, you either have no preference or prefer the lower suit—it would deny a strong preference for the higher suit.

		WEST	NORTH	EAST	SOUTH
♠ 10 7 4			1♡	No	1NT
♡ A J 9 4 3		No	No	No	
◇ Q 4					
♣ A J 7					

♠ A Q 9 5
♡ 6
◇ 8 7 3 2
♣ Q 10 6 2

West leads ♣2: seven, king, five. East returns ♣8: nine, six, jack. (West could follow safely with the *queen* of clubs as a secondary signal.) The play continues as follows:

3. ◇Q from dummy: king, ace, eight
4. ♡5 from declarer: six, nine, queen
5. ♣4 from East: three, queen (signal for spades), ace
6. ♡3 from dummy: East wins the king, South playing the 7
7. ♠2 from East: six, queen, four
8. West cashes the ♣Q: ♠7 from dummy, ♡8 from East, ◇5 from South. How should West continue?

East's ♡8 is a significant card. South must have three hearts. East cannot have the ♡10 because East won with the king at trick 6 and so East began with K-Q-8-2 and South with 10-7-5. (With four hearts, South would have raised to 2♡.) The ♡8 discard, the higher heart, asks West to play the higher suit.

West should play the ♠A next. East held: ♠J832 ♡KQ82 ◇K10 ♣K84 and South had ♠K6 ♡1075 ◇AJ965 ♣953.

On the ♠A and spade continuation, 1NT is two off, while on a 'safe' diamond exit, declarer will succeed.

TIP 100:

Red on red. Black on black.

If all players were perfect, there would never be any silly mistakes. In real life, however, we are not robots but are human and prone to human failings. A good defender can exploit such weaknesses and one method is to prey on a lapse of concentration when declarer is drawing trumps or tackling a long suit. If you are out of the suit declarer is leading, play a card of the same colour. If hearts are trumps, 'follow' with a diamond: if declarer is playing spades, discard a club. This m꜡ cause an insufficiently alert declarer to miscount the suit.

Naturally you use red on red, black on black only when you have no important signal to send and you can spare a card in the suit of the same colour. Of course it will almost never work against an expert and it will rarely work early in a session, but after about three hours of play, many a player's mental energy has been known to wilt. Seeing a card of the same colour, it is easy to assume a player has followed suit. How often have you heard a declarer say, 'I thought all the trumps had gone', possibly another victim of red on red, black on black.

Red on black. Black on red.

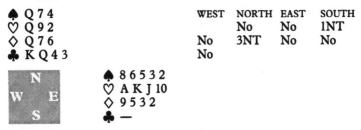

	WEST	NORTH	EAST	SOUTH
♠ Q 7 4		No	No	1NT
♡ Q 9 2				
◇ Q 7 6	No	3NT	No	No
♣ K Q 4 3	No			

♠ 8 6 5 3 2
♡ A K J 10
◇ 9 5 3 2
♣ —

West leads ♣5. What should East discard?

With standard signals, East should plan to throw the 2 of spades and the 2 of diamonds. By discouraging both those suits, you should be able to transmit the message that you want hearts. Discard the 2 of diamonds first, red on black.

Just as you play red on red, black on black to have declarer miss your card, so you play a card of the opposite colour when you want to wake partner up to the fact that you are not following suit. Partner should not need such a jolt, but we all know what partners are really like, don't we?

Happy bridging!